William Faulkner

WILLIAM FAULKNER

by FREDERICK J. HOFFMAN

TWAYNE PUBLISHERS
A DIVISION OF G. K. HALL & CO., BOSTON

William Faulkner, Second Edition Revised

Frederick J. Hoffman

First edition copyright © 1961 by Twayne Publishers, Inc.
Second edition including new and revised material
copyright © 1966 by Twayne Publishers, Inc.
All Rights Reserved

Twayne Publishers
A Division of G. K. Hall & Co.
70 Lincoln Street
Boston, Massachusetts 02111

Manufactured in the United States of America

First Paperback Edition, 1985

Library of Congress Catalog Card Number: 61–9856

ISBN 0–8057–0244–X
ISBN 0–8057–7444–0 (pbk.)

To EC and CE

Contents

About the Author

Frederick J. Hoffman is professor of Modern Literature at the University of California, Riverside. Born in Wisconsin, he was educated at Stanford University, the University of Minnesota, and The Ohio State University. He has taught at the universities of Chicago, Wisconsin, Oklahoma, and Washington, at The Ohio State University, and at Harvard. In 1953-1954, he was visiting Fulbright Professor at the Universities of Rennes and Grenoble, France, and lectured as well in Rome, Nice, and at the Sorbonne in Paris.

In addition to the present book, he is author of *Freudianism and the Literary Mind, The Modern Novel in America, The Twenties,* and *Gertrude Stein;* co-author of *The Little Magazine;* co-editor of *William Faulkner: Three Decades of Criticism, The Achievement of D. H. Lawrence,* and *The Growth of American Literature.* At present he is at work on an exhaustive study of the perspectives upon death in modern literature. He is an editor of *PMLA* and editorial advisor in the area of modern fiction, *College English.*

Preface

THE FIRST chapter of *William Faulkner* offers several important perspectives upon Faulkner's work as a whole. The study of his uses of time is also by implication an analysis of a major characteristic of his style. In the light of what has happened in both Faulkner's fiction and the criticism of him in the 1950's, this study of his approach to his characters, his uses of them, and their role in the general strategy of his fiction is of special value.

Successive chapters, II through VI, present the novels in the order of their publication. Since the emphasis is on the major works, each chapter considers two or three of them within a thematic and conceptual framework. In Chapter II I discuss the work of Faulkner's "apprenticeship" and indicate the ways his first publications anticipate themes and sentiments of the later work. The chapter concludes with a consideration of *Sartoris*, the first of the Yoknapatawpha novels.

Chapter III is a study of two of Faulkner's major works, *The Sound and the Fury* and *As I Lay Dying*, which are significant contributions to the art of modern fiction and substantial parts of the Yoknapatawpha design. The discussion stresses the aesthetic implications of Faulkner's experiments in narrative perspective and their effect upon his conceptions of characters and human events.

In Chapter III, the account considers Faulkner's several ways of treating the problem of evil as manifested in man, in group society, and in the natural dispositions toward violence and extremes of passion. The texts emphasized in this chapter are *Sanctuary, Light in August,* and *Absalom, Absalom!*

Chapter IV has as its major area the problems of "the folk" and of the Negro in Faulkner's world—in other words, the problem of man in two major forms. *Go Down, Moses, Intruder in the Dust* and *The Hamlet* are the most significant texts. There is, of course, much discussion of related matters: Faulkner's humor, his various attempts to explore the figure of the "leader who fails," his attempts to distinguish between morality in the abstract and concrete purposeful action.

The final chapter presents the Faulkner of the last decade. In *Requiem for a Nun, A Fable,* and other recent works, he struggles with the problems of rhetoric and forceful moral statement—and with the difficulties caused by them in the creation of works of art. I try to suggest not only the continuity of the early with the more recent work but also the differences of style, characterization, and meaning between these two phases of his career.

Perhaps the principal virtue of this book—aside from its treatments of the individual works—is that it benefits from the perspective provided by the mature state both of Faulkner's career and of the criticism. Thus the post-Nobel Faulkner is judged in terms of his early career; the great work to 1950 is reviewed from the vantage point of the early 1960's. These two views—an advantage earlier studies of Faulkner, of course, did not have—make it evident that the major difference of the fiction of the two periods is in manner of presentation: what is implicit, or dramatized, in the great novels of "the time of genius" becomes explicit in a special, very interesting way after 1950. I have tried to assess this difference in Chapter VI.

It is also important to see that Faulkner's own statements about his fiction, now quite fully and elaborately offered in several books and articles, do not on the whole neglect the early work; nor do they present him as a literary pundit. The total impression of Faulkner is that he has produced a series of writings of immense skill and importance, which possess a remarkable thematic unity and a great variety of precise representations of the human comedy. I have tried to show the forms of unity in chapters I and VI and to present the variety, richness and scope of his imagination in II-V.

The appendixes offer other assistance to the reader. The bibliography begins with a checklist of Faulkner's works; beyond that, it mentions only those book-length studies in English that have a distinct value; the uses of each are specified. The notes provide additional commentary and cross-references, and they refer to the extensive body of Faulkner criticism now available. There is also a brief chronology, which sets the book within the perspective of significant dates of Faulkner's life.

The purpose of *William Faulkner* is to provide maximum information in minimum space. The book is quite frankly an introduction—a reading of the major novels, with some suggestions of the place of the lesser ones—which also indicates Faulkner's importance for us: his ability to define many significant aspects of the human condition, without being caught very often in the act of making superficial judgments or abstractions. His superb sense of human and natural detail is combined with a deep and an intricate exploration of human psychology. Except for a few recent lapses, he does not lose sight of the fact that human truth in literature necessitates a creative attention to the particulars of the human condition. His work at its best is a remarkable fusion of humor, comedy, psychological insight, violence, and tragedy. When it achieves a balance of these characteristics, it joins company with the greatest achievements in modern literature. My study of his novels should testify to my pleasure in his accomplishment and to my recognition of the thematic and symbolic values.

I should like to express my gratitude to Sylvia Bowman, whose admirable editing of copy saved me many mistakes. If others remain, they are solely my responsibility.

FREDERICK J. HOFFMAN

The University of California
Riverside
September 16, 1960

PREFACE TO THE 1966 EDITION

Several considerations have prompted this new edition of *William Faulkner*. For one thing, Faulkner's death on July 6, 1962, both requires and permits at least a semi-definitive reappraisal. Also, the publication in 1962 of *The Reivers* demands an additional comment. Finally, the scope and range of Faulkner scholarship and criticism have immensely increased in the last few years. I have noted some of this increase in an expanded checklist.

I have also made a number of changes. My discussion of *The Reivers* replaces Part IV of Chapter Six of the first edition; I have added a new chapter (Seven) to the book, to provide a further summing up of Faulkner's work, so that chapters One and Seven are now opening and concluding perspectives on the Faulkner world. The new checklist accounts for books and pamphlets on Faulkner, all but one in English; the exception is an especially useful study in French. Finally, I have made a few corrections in the text, and additions to it whenever the new circumstances required them.

As was the case with the first edition, this book remains an introduction to its subject. It makes no pretense of being thorough or original, except in such cases as I have applied my own insights to the criticism of the novels. A book of this kind should inform the reader who is a beginner and provide what my original Preface claimed, that is, "the maximum information in minimum space." Thanks to the editor and the publisher of TUSAS, I have been able to increase that minimum by a number of pages. I hope that I have taken full advantage of the opportunity to increase the usefulness of the book.

The author thanks the following publishers for permission to quote from Faulkner's works: The Liveright Publishing Company for permission to quote 51 words from *Mosquitoes;* Random House, for all other quotations. Specific acknowledgments are indicated in the place of quotation.

Frederick J. Hoffman

Riverside, California

Chronology

1825   July 6, birth of William C. Falkner, great-grandfather, Knox County, Tennessee (his life basis of many incidents used in Faulkner's work).

1872   The Ripley, Ship Island, and Kentucky Railroad completed by Colonel Falkner and his partner, R. J. Thurmond.

1881   *The White Rose of Memphis*, by Colonel Falkner, published in book form, first of thirty-seven editions (most recent in 1953).

1889   W. C. Falkner killed by J. S. Thurmond, streets of Ripley, Mississippi. See T. F. Hickerson, *The Falkner Feuds* (Chapel Hill, N.C.: Colonial Press, 1964).

1897   September 25, William Falkner born, New Albany, Mississippi: parents, Murray C. and Maud Butler Falkner.

1902   Move to Oxford, Mississippi.

1914   Friendship with Phil Stone begins.

1918   July 8, to Toronto, for training in British RAF; made an honorary second lieutenant, December 22.

1919   September, Faulkner enrolled at University of Mississippi as special student. August 6, a poem, "L'Aprés-Midi d'un Faune," published in the *New Republic*.

1920   November, withdrew from University of Mississippi; trip to New York, on invitation of Stark Young.

1922-   Faulkner in Oxford, odd jobs, finally as postmaster for
1924   the University station. Resigned from job, 1924.

1924   First book published: *The Marble Faun*, a book of poems, published by the Four Seas Company of Boston.

1925   Lived for six months in New Orleans, during which time contributed sixteen signed stories and sketches to the Sunday feature section of the New Orleans *Times-Picayune* (eleven of these published as *Mirrors of Chartres Street*, 1953; all sixteen published as *New Orleans Sketches*, 1955); also contributions to New Orleans little magazine, the *Double Dealer* (these published as *Salmagundi*, 1932). Friendship with Sherwood Anderson, discussions of writing. June: shipped for Europe on the freighter, *West Ivis*. Returned to Oxford, late in the year.

1926   *Sherwood Anderson and Other Famous Creoles* published, containing a parody of Anderson, which caused a halt in friendship with Faulkner.

1929   Publication of *Sartoris* (January) and *The Sound and the Fury* (October), first novels of Yoknapatawpha. Married Estelle Oldham Franklin.

1932   November, to Hollywood, as script writer and advisor; continued intermittently after May, 1933.

1939   Essay by George M. O'Donnell in *Kenyon Review*, first mature appraisal of his work as a whole.

1946   Publication of the Viking *Portable Faulkner*, beginning of fresh appraisals of his work.

1949   Advised in filming of *Intruder in the Dust*, Lafayette County and Oxford, Mississippi.

1950   December, to Stockholm, to accept 1949 Nobel Prize for Literature. (His speech published by the Spiral Press, New York, March, 1951.)

1951   Presented .with L'Ordre National de la Légion d'Honneur, New Orleans. Also given National Book Award for *Collected Stories*.

1952   May, Faulkner welcomed by the French at the Salle Gaveau, Paris, in connection with the festival, *Oeuvres de XXe Siècle*.

1955   August, trip to Japan for conferences and lectures, Nagano and elsewhere (See *Faulkner at Nagano*). Won Pulitzer Prize and National Book Award, for *The Fable*.

1956   September 20, Albert Camus adaptation of *Requiem for a Nun* opened in Paris.

1957-   Two semesters as Writer-in-Residence, University of
1958   Virginia (February to June, 1957; February to June, 1958). (See *Faulkner in the University*.)

1962   July 6, Faulkner died of heart attack.

1963   Awarded Pulitzer Prize posthumously, for *The Reivers*.

CHAPTER 1

Introduction: Time and Space

I

IN THE ALMOST forty years since he first published a volume of poems, *The Marble Faun* (1924), William Faulkner has emerged from obscurity to a position of world eminence as perhaps the best known of all modern American writers. In December of 1950 he was awarded the Nobel Prize for Literature and, in the decade following, was called upon many times to state his views and to explain his work. His is probably not so unusual a story except for the fact that the period of obscurity was a long one; Faulkner had to overcome many obstacles to win widespread popular acceptance.

A number of circumstances made his success possible. He wrote from and about a part of the country that has always fascinated readers the world over; the South has its own sources of profound interest, and Faulkner soon became known as pre-eminently a "novelist of the South." More important, he succeeded both in going beyond the superficial record of the South as a unique, historical region and in presenting a profound analysis of universal human problems. In the years since 1950, Faulkner has been "rediscovered" as a man peculiarly suited to the examination of specifically modern aspects of the human situation. Perhaps most significant of all is his power of concentration, his ability to bring his fictional world to such a level of imaginative realization that it proves to be more actual than the real. He is as preoccupied with the detailed, specific qualities of that world as Balzac was with his. The creatures of his imagination are endowed with such intensity and vividness of representation that their world becomes absolutely convincing.

Faulkner's career essentially comprehends three principal phases: the usual time of apprenticeship (1924–1929), when he tried to make up his mind if he would become a writer and what kind he should be; the "time of genius" (1929–1936), when he not only settled upon his "trade" and his subject, but produced the most remarkable series of first-rate novels ever written by a single person in so short a time; and the period of "consolidation and affirmation" (1940 to the present), when the presentation of Yoknapatawpha County[1] was enriched and elaborated upon and when Faulkner pushed far beyond it to attempt a statement of universal truths.

The period of apprenticeship produced only three works. These are interesting primarily for what they say of a young man groping for a style and a subject: a volume of poems, *The Marble Faun* (1924), notable for echoes of late nineteenth century mannerisms; a novel in the postwar tradition, *Soldiers' Pay* (1926), which reflects the current interest in postwar disillusion; and a novel, *Mosquitoes* (1927), that seems at least superficially an imitation of Aldous Huxley whose *Point Counterpoint* (1928) impressed many contemporaries as a masterful summary of postwar attitudes. Each of these works is obviously in its own way an uneasy pose and affectation. Faulkner was conscious of the attractive possibilities of genius, but had not yet decided upon a place or a function for his talent, nor indeed been certain whether he had a talent.

In 1925 he wrote for a New Orleans "little magazine," the *Double Dealer*, that immediately after the war he was entirely unsure what direction his career would take. In Oxford, Mississippi, he said, ". . . I read and employed verse, firstly, for the purpose of furthering various philanderings in which I was engaged, secondly, to complete a youthful gesture I was then making of being different in a small town."[2]

The net result of Faulkner's postwar years was, however,

more substantial than his statement suggests; but it was not representative of the man who has become a major novelist in our time. Besides the three books, he published some sixteen stories and sketches (1925) in the New Orleans *Times Picayune*; these have been collected and edited by Carvel Collins under the title, *William Faulkner: New Orleans Sketches.*³ Their value, like that of most other early books, seems now fairly well admitted to be in their suggestions and anticipations of the major works.

These major works of the "time of genius" began in 1929. *Sartoris* was the first indication that Faulkner had settled upon both a place and a manner for his work. In the very same year appeared *The Sound and the Fury*, one of the most important novels of the century. These two were followed by *As I Lay Dying* (1930) and *Sanctuary* (1931), both written quickly and as "*tours de force*."⁴ In 1932, *Light in August* followed, and in 1936, *Absalom, Absalom!*

These six novels are the core of Faulkner's major achievement. They introduce the special world of Yoknapatawpha County; they offer an already elaborate description of its topography and its people; and they are a brilliant beginning of Faulkner's profound analyses of the human moral condition, for which he is now justly known and admired. In range of style and structure, in the power of analysis of character, and in the sheer brilliance and versatility of literary accomplishment, they are not equalled anywhere in modern American literature.

There were other, relatively minor works between 1936 and 1940, the beginning of the third major phase. The novel *Pylon* (1935) is much admired in England and in Europe, but not otherwise considered a great success. *The Unvanquished* (1938), a unified series of stories concerning Bayard Sartoris and his growth to maturity, has interest and great charm; and it is often recommended as the "easiest" beginning for the reader unaccustomed to Faulkner's more difficult works. *The Wild Palms* (1939) is a complex novel which attempts to fuse two separate but thematically interrelated stories.⁵

The third important phase of his career—the period of "consolidation and affirmation"—begins in 1940, with the publication of *The Hamlet*. There are three clearly noticeable subdivisions: the Snopes saga, which comprehends *The Hamlet*, *The Town* (1957) and *The Mansion* (1959); the works that are specifically concerned with the Negro as a race, a group, and a moral problem—*Go Down, Moses* (1942), *Intruder in the Dust* (1948); and the books in which he has tried, through one or another device, to make a clear, affirmative statement concerning the "eternal verities" and man's responsible trust. In these novels, Faulkner has tried two devices: a moral spokesman, Gavin Stevens, who at times appears to speak almost directly for his author in *Intruder in the Dust*, *Knight's Gambit* (1949), and *Requiem for a Nun* (1951); and an elaborate parable or allegory in *A Fable* (1954), in which the assertions of the Stockholm address of 1950 are dramatized.

These preliminary facts should impress one at least with one truth: the time of Faulkner's greatest work coincided with his decision to take the place where he had lived and which he knew best and to present it in depth and variety. The place was Faulkner's Oxford, Mississippi, and its county and immediate surrounding land, in the northwestern part of the state. Here he has lived from 1902 on (he was born in New Albany, Mississippi, in 1897), despite some absences. During the first World War he managed to get as far as Canada; after the war, he stayed in New Orleans, New York, and Europe for short periods; and after his recognition by the Nobel Prize Committee, he lectured and taught in various places in the country (The University of Virginia, for one) and abroad (Japan in 1955, for example).

Early in 1956 in the best of several interviews, Faulkner described to Jean Stein his "invention" of Yoknapatawpha County and his use of it since 1929 in his fiction:

With *Soldiers' Pay* I found out writing was fun. But I found out afterward that not only each book had to have a design but the whole output or sum of an artist's work had to have a design. With *Soldiers' Pay* and *Mosquitoes* I wrote for the sake of writing because it was fun. Beginning with *Sartoris* I discovered that my own little postage stamp of native soil was worth writing about and that I would never live long enough to exhaust it, and that by sublimating the actual into the apocryphal I would have complete liberty to use whatever talent I might have to its absolute top. It opened up a gold mine of other people, so I created a cosmos of my own. I can move these people around like God, not only in space but in time too. The fact that I have moved my characters around in time successfully, at least in my own estimation, proves to me my own theory that time is a fluid condition which has no existence except in the momentary avatars of individual people. There is no such thing as *was*—only *is*. If *was* existed, there would be no grief or sorrow. I like to think of the world I created as being a kind of keystone in the universe; that, small as that keystone is, if it were taken away the universe would itself collapse. . . .[6]

These remarks suggest, among many other things, the one clear truth that Faulkner believed his own best knowledge of people and place to be the soundest source of imaginative invention. Oxford, Ripley, and Holly Springs were from time to time recreated as Jefferson; and Lafayette County and neighboring areas served as the models of Yoknapatawpha; but they also became, as he says, "a cosmos of my own" through the agency of his vivid and intense power to create the aesthetically real from the place and character of experience. The major reason for Faulkner's eminence is that he had this opportunity, from long acquaintance, to make his "own little postage stamp of native soil" a genuinely convincing setting for the elaborate development of a moral fable and legend of universal human circumstance.

Faulkner had the additional advantage of a heritage, so that not only place but time was available to his consciousness. The "legend" of the County also embraced tradition and history because he was himself an heir of both in the affairs of the Falkner family.[7] His great-grandfather, William C. Falkner, was a colonel in the Civil War, supervised the building of a railroad in the years following, and was finally killed in 1889 by a business rival, J. H. Thurmond. Falkner was a curious mixture of the practical and the romantic in post-Civil War history. As Robert Cantwell states in his informative essay on Faulkner's ancestry, the Colonel belonged in the category of the "businessman who tried to carry into industry the code of the landed aristocracy, a plantation owner who combined with Southern traditions the spirit of enterprise, too entangled with the Old South to detach himself intellectually from it, and too intelligent to accept it completely. . . ."[8] Colonel Falkner was also an author, and, in the case of one of his three books, a popular one; his novel, *The White Rose of Memphis* (1881) achieved thirty-five editions and sold 160,000 copies.

Faulkner's family past seems, therefore, to have done for tradition in his fiction what the town of Oxford did for its particular facts of place and social strata in the Yoknapatawpha novels. But both past and present, both time and space, are to be seen in them, not as actual or reportorial, but as imaginative reconstructions. Time, Faulkner said, does not exist except "in the momentary avatars of individual people." What impresses any careful reader of Faulkner's work is, therefore, its intensity of concentration. Faulkner in actual life was a citizen of his world and his region; but, as an author, he was a creator who could, as he said to Miss Stein, "move these people around like God, not only in space but in time too." The distinction between citizen and creator cannot be emphasized enough. Yoknapatawpha is not "real," though it is invested with a superb sense of imaginary reality on the level of the created world. Of Yoknapatawpha he was "Sole Owner & Proprietor," as he reminded us in the end-papers of *Absalom, Absalom!*

This remarkable, regional creation is in the gullied, eroded, red-clay country, some seventy-five miles south of Memphis, in the Delta country of northern Mississippi. The County is bordered on the north by the Tallahatchie River; on the south, by the Yoknapatawpha. Two gravel and dirt roads, in a cruciform design, intersect at Jefferson, the county seat. The Sartoris-built railroad, pointing to Memphis Junction, runs parallel to the north-south road. Two other roads feed diagonally into the town, one from the fishing and hunting country and from the "Sutpen's Hundred" of one hundred square miles (*Absalom, Absalom!*), the other from the village of Frenchman's Bend where Flem Snopes began his career (*The Hamlet*).

The map is rich in Faulknerian detail; every place in it has a role in the complex saga of the County. Yet the whole is treated with the scrupulous objectivity of a surveyor. The county has 2400 square miles. Its population, as of 1936, is 15,611: "Whites, 6298; Negroes, 9313." This numerical superiority of Negroes has its own significance throughout Faulkner's work. It becomes a "problem" from the beginning, but it is treated with great sublety—not as a mathematical or an economic issue, but as a sign of racial, social, and ultimately moral differentiation.

The truth is that this richly endowed "postage stamp of native soil" is the point of departure for a moral fable of the condition of man, both American and universal. Both the people and the landscape are presented with the most meticulous care for accuracy and fullness of detail. We are never entirely lost in generalities, even though each character unites in himself precise detail and suggestions of universality. The created world is superior to its source in geographical reality because of the emotional and rhetorical intensity with which Faulkner approaches it. That its people and their habitation reflect their regional source is not important. Faulkner's genius is not concerned with discussing a "representative world" of specimens and types. Classes of people, economic strata, political maneuvering are not important. Rather, the details of Yoknapatawpha's life, recorded with such an obsessive diligence, are only the means of a deep examination of the urgent drives and the moral imperatives of man: Irving Howe calls his work "a moral fable of which the materials derive from Southern life but the meanings—at Faulkner's best—are quite without geographical reference or limit. . . ."[9]

II

Of the many ways of presenting the major thematic concerns in Faulkner's work, I have chosen two in the hope that they will help us to see his fiction as a whole before we examine separate examples. The first of these has to do with Faulkner's treatment of time (including historical time, tradition, as well as narrative rhythm and pace); the second is an attempt to show the gradual change in Faulkner's management and use of central character as a reflection of his interest in implicit and explicit statement. As for the first of these, it is probably the most important approach one may make to Faulkner. While a literal, lineal time has no place of appreciable significance in Faulkner's work, the pressure of past upon present is seen in a variety of complex and interesting ways as affecting the psychology and morality of individual actions.

I shall begin by offering a diagram of the several time patterns in Faulkner's work. It is an oversimplification, but it should help as a point of departure in the discussion.

A. Edenic Past	B. Actual Past	C. Major Event	D. ("Was") Recent	E. Present
No historical time	1699-1960	1861-65	Past	("Is") 1920 +

This sketch demands several preliminary observations. The "Edenic time" (A) is a pre-historical or a non-historical time, or a non-temporal existence, a point before or beyond time, when active moral criteria either have not yet entered human history or are not really contained within the human consciousness. The "actual past" (B) means the beginning of recorded history—that is, within Faulkner's record; the earliest specific date mentioned by him is 1699, a date given in the 1946 appendix of *The Sound and the Fury*. But the developing time is largely emphasized as within the nineteenth century, leading toward and away from the "Major Event" (C), the

Civil War, in which the accumulated tensions and moral crises received a catastrophic and a significantly violent expression. This does not mean that Faulkner is an "historical novelist," nor that he gives the Civil War much specific attention (it plays a large role only in *The Unvanquished* and is cited at some length otherwise in *Sartoris, Light in August,* and *Absalom, Absalom!*). The most important use of time in Faulkner is the pattern or movement of it—largely in the consciousness of his characters, not in terms of narrative exposition—from this major event through the Recent Past (*D*) to the Present (*E*). This movement is reciprocal, and it alternates in terms of symbol and forms of psychological reaction, so that there is much shifting back and forth between *C* and *E*, in what he calls "the momentary avatars of individual people."

There is, of course, an historical pattern in Faulkner's work, but it has to be picked up from here and there in the novels and stories; it is not presented as a straightforward chronology. In 1946 Malcolm Cowley (with Faulkner's assistance, or at least with his approval) tried his hand at a reconstruction of the Yoknapatawpha past when he edited the Viking *Portable Faulkner.* He began with the pre-Civil War time, from 1820–1859, showing the Indian-Negro exploitation and their replacement by white Southerners. The Civil War is then represented by two selections from *The Unvanquished;* and the time from 1865 to 1900 is portrayed in the loss of a tradition and the destruction of the wilderness ("The Bear" is the obvious example to use here). Finally, the twentieth century is represented in stories of the emergence of the Snopes tribe and what Cowley calls "The End of an Order"—the decline of substantial families, the evidences of decay, etc. The saga concludes with an excerpt from *Go Down, Moses,* called "Delta Autumn," in which Ike McCaslin mourns the passing of a primitive world, a wilderness which had been hacked away and, as Faulkner says in "The Bear," "constantly and punily gnawed at by men with plows and axes who feared it because it was wilderness. . . ."[10] Cowley's is a fascinating and an ingenious design, but it is also a distortion of Faulkner's uses of time because it is too neat and too clear and because it ignores his major use of the relationship of past and present, which is psychological and not historical.

Above all, the reader must understand that Faulkner sees time in a complex of human tensions and as fully absorbed in and integrated with rhetoric, style, and narrative pace and rhythm. The reader is almost never aware of a pure present (*Sanctuary* is a conspicuous exception; occasionally other novels isolate the present, but only momentarily); nor is a *specific past* very often exclusively given. There are two important, typical uses of time in the novels: the slow, gradual, painstaking reconstruction of the past by narrators who exist in the present or existed in the recent past (as in *Absalom*); and the pattern of movement from past to present to past, or within points in the past (*The Sound and the Fury* is a good example). In either case, one almost never sees the present as a pure or separate time; it is infused with the past, it has meaning only in terms of it, and its complex nature results from the fusion of the two.

One may describe Faulknerian time as a continuum: time flowing from past into present and from present into past. Reality is not so much objective existence but what past and present have made of an object or an event within a given set of psychological conditions. Reality thus becomes, as Karl Zink has described it, . . .

> less a matter of time and space than a condition of the consciousness. Faulkner recognizes and dramatizes a vital distinction between simple, clock or calendar, time which is man's chronology of the flow of change, and a "pure" Time. Simple time is a measuring device, and "pure" Time is experience, coextensive with the individual consciousness; it is not a chronology so much as it is a continuous attempt to assess real value.[11]

Besides this very important view of time, there is the idea of an "Edenic past" (*A* of the above diagram). This may be called pure stasis or a timeless vision or an unhistorical condition existing before and transcending human complication. In various ways it is described (and glimpsed briefly) in "The Bear," *Absalom, Light in August, Requiem for a Nun,* and in numerous brief images elsewhere. Irving Howe (*Faulkner,* 66) calls it "a past removed from historical time, an Eden coexisting with society yet never mistaken for society by those who come to it for refreshment and purification." Perhaps its nature and the contrasting symbol of historical obsession can be seen in Byron Bunch of *Light in August,* who moves at first unsteadily between Gail Hightower, a supreme example of the obsessive soul fixed in a static symbol of the historical past, and Lena Grove, whose existence in "pure" Edenic time is marked by her absolute immunity from the stresses and strains of human involvement. Bunch finally goes with Lena and becomes a kind of secular "Joseph" companion of her backwoods Madonna and child.

This vision of an Edenic past is one of the more substantial in American literature. The "state of innocence" which antedates or ignores or avoids experience is in one way or another expressed as a point of reference for a major journey of the American personality from innocence to experience. As Henry Nash Smith has abundantly proved in *The Virgin Land* (1950), it was one of the most frequently employed images on the frontier. Its many literary variations include James Fenimore Cooper's Leather-Stocking tales, Mark Twain's *The Adventures of Huckleberry Finn,* the Nick Adams of Hemingway's *In Our Time* and stories of other volumes, and such cruder uses of it as Sherwood Anderson's *Dark Laughter* and Waldo Frank's *Holiday.*[12]

In Faulkner's novels, the figure of the Edenic past is symbolized variously in the wilderness of "The Bear"; in the state of pre-historical innocence described in *Absalom;* and in the vision of the arrested, static, still reality of the road to Jefferson in the first chapter of *Light in August* and of the landscape of the farm beyond Jefferson in *Intruder in the Dust.*

Faulkner's language also has an especial relevance to this kind of "still moment": the words *motionless, arrested, frozen, suspended, immobile, soporific,* and others define the condition of static innocence. The following passage, from *Intruder in the Dust,* illustrates the effect upon Faulkner's rhetoric:

> . . . there should have been fixed in monotonous repetition the land's living symbol—a formal group of ritual almost mystic significance identical and monotonous as milestones tying the county-seat to the county's ultimate rim as milestones would: the beast the plow and the man integrated in one foundationed into the frozen wave of their furrow tremendous with effort yet at the same same vacant of progress, ponderable immovable and immobile like groups of wrestling statuary set against the land's immensity. . .[13]

This rhetoric, and many figures like it, is used to define an arrest of consciousness, a state of suspension; in many cases it also suggests an "ideal" state of nature which precedes the onrushing of time, the beginning of "progress" and decay in human affairs. In most examples, there is an implicit criticism of the nature of human evil or vileness or sheer moral insensibility. But it would be a serious mistake to assume from this that Faulkner is a "primitivist": that he counsels a retreat from the present to an ideal, undefiled state of nature.

In many respects, the quality of Edenic stillness is also a matter of characterization and description; the hero in Faulkner frequently matches stillness against violence. He is sometimes badly mistaken in so doing, or at any rate Faulkner seems to suggest that neither of the extremes of Quentin Compson and his father is feasible or workable. The Edenic past is a form of representing a state of nature, both a descriptive and a normative means of defining the role and the effect of man's effect upon it and upon history.

Gavin Stevens says at one point in *Intruder in the Dust* that time is "all man had, . . . all that stood between him and the death he feared and abhorred. . . ." There is much in Faulkner's novels of this kind of tension. His characters are intense creatures, obsessed with their isolation in the world, abnormally puzzled over the character and degree of the burdens they must assume, and desperate to assert themselves before death closes in on them. In this respect, the complex of past and present, assuming both the "burdens" of history and the struggle of self-definition, becomes a means of classifying Faulkner's characters. A not uncommon type of struggle in his novels is, therefore, that against the threat and menace of time—a struggle to put a stop to time and to prevent it from defiling an ideal.

This condition of an obsessive forcing of human history is most effectively shown in the debate going on in Quentin Compson's mind (as he prepares to go to his suicide) with the memory of his father's past advices and observations: ". . . and he you wanted to sublimate a piece of natural human folly into a horror and then exorcise it with truth and i it was to isolate her out of the loud world so that it would have to flee us of necessity. . . ."[14] Quentin tries every means to destroy time, to disprove its accuracy and its effective control of human affairs because it is a ˙testimony and a measurement of human decay.

In contrast, the Negro servant Dilsey is able to adjust to time and history without permitting them to defeat her; her ideal belief in universals is, therefore, much more genuine and more "enduring" than Quentin's. This beautiful detail from Part IV of *The Sound and the Fury*, shows Dilsey's reaction to time while in the kitchen of the Compson home on Easter Sunday morning:

> On the wall above a cupboard, invisible save at night, by lamp light and even evincing an enigmatic profundity because it had but one hand, a cabinet clock ticked, then with a preliminary sound as if it had cleared its throat, struck five times.
> "Eight o'clock," Dilsey said . . . (290).

She is entirely at home in the erratic world and has calculated accurately the proper balance of errors within it. She is therefore able, beyond the power of any of the Compsons whom she has served for many decades, to balance the real against the ideal and to "endure" beyond the collapse of the family she has served.

Quentin's attempt to fix time is only one of Faulkner's examples; perhaps the most obvious is the cliché reaction or stock response to human event. Men and women give labels to events unthinkingly and irresponsibly, and this tendency is an example of meeting evasively the moral burden of the past. Faulkner most successfully contrasts this cliché with the problem of man himself: the abstraction "nigger" is forced to meet the test of the vitality of "man." This situation is the dramatic substance of *Intruder in the Dust*: Lucas Beauchamp —as Negro and as Man—is a constant challenge not only to the general run of townspeople in Jefferson but also to the young hero, Chick Mallison. Chick must eventually recognize Lucas's manhood as opposed to the abstract expectations of his "niggerhood" that are a part of the cultural prejudice he has inherited. Beyond this relationship, there is the more immediate crisis of the mob who, like the one gathered about Joanna Burden's burning house in *Light in August*, wish to act on a fixed stereotype idea of Negro-evil-punishment. Chick's role is not only to prove Lucas innocent of murder, but also to convince himself that the stereotype is ineffectual; this accomplished, the mob (which Faulkner identifies as "The Face") dissolves, disappears; and the human truth triumphs over the abstract label.

Besides these manipulations of time as abstract versus time as "real," there are five other ways in which Faulkner describes the relationship of the individual to the past. On occasions the Faulkner character assumes the burden of the past in an obsessive way: Joe Christmas, at first puzzled, then goaded into defying the social status created by his being called Negro, finally forced himself into the role of martyr-victim and died at the hands of Percy Grimm, a similarly extreme but less convincing example of obsessive singleness of desire and purpose.

In another example, the Faulkner hero drives relentlessly toward the accomplishment of an abstract "design." Thomas Sutpen of *Absalom* begins outside time, in a version of Edenic peace and freedom, he then encounters the world, its privileges and its offensive inequities; and he tries to impose his will on time by forcefully determining a world and a place for himself in Southern society. In so doing, he violates natural and human rhythms; this is the real "flaw" in his design, or we may say that the design is itself a master flaw, a curiously Faulknerian example of the Greek *hubris*.

In a third example of the individual's reaction to time, we have the hero who is "trapped in history"—immobilized because of a fixation in the past. The obvious example is Gail Hightower of *Light in August,* whose immobility is very different from having "endured time," as Dilsey has; it comes from an absolute dedication to a mistaken view of history and heroism. Hightower's vision of a Civil War cavalry charge which involves his grandfather, but is actually a trivial and vulgar detail, pursues him throughout his life and paralyzes him for living; he is almost never able to rescue himself from it, even temporarily, effectively to rejoin the human race. The vision is presented to him in the symbol of an ever-turning wheel:

> . . . It spins now, fading, without progress, as though turned by that final flood which had rushed out of him, leaving his body empty and lighter than a forgotten leaf and even more trivial than flotsam lying spent and still upon the window ledge . . .[15]

The fourth kind of available reaction to time is to deny that the past exists. The reverse of assuming that only it exists, it is a psychological variant upon the obsessed figure who tries to order the world in his own image. Examples of this type are rare, and in a sense only Popeye of *Sanctuary* is entirely suitable. He is an unrelieved, grotesque figure of the "mechanical" present. The opening description of him sets the tone, which is maintained throughout:

> . . . His face had a queer, bloodless color, as though seen by electric light; against the sunny silence, in his slanted straw hat and his slightly akimbo arms, he had that vicious depthless quality of stamped tin.[16]

Finally, the Faulkner character may adopt a simple vision of the past, setting aside its extreme aberrations and resting trustfully upon its promise of stability and endurance. This fifth class of response to time is truly complex, and it involves many variants. There is the "Edenic vision," discussed above; there is the steady, balanced "acceptance" of time and its erosive effect upon man, practiced so effectively by Dilsey; there is the practical, ready adaptation to circumstances of Cash in *As I Lay Dying*. There are many such characters in Faulkner's work who often seem his "reserve" of stability: old Miss Habersham of *Intruder;* Lena Grove of *Light in August;* Sam Fathers and Ike McCaslin of "The Bear"; and many of the Negroes throughout his fiction. As Karl Zink said in "Faulkner's Garden," Negroes, women, and children often possess a "spiritual equilibrium" which his major heroes often lack:

> . . . Despite their poverty and depressed status, the Negroes have a spiritual equilibrium as people who live on and by the old earth, cherishing their families, protecting the young.[17]

III

The final introductory approach to Faulkner's work as a whole carries a risk of over-simplification similar to that of the others I have used; yet, if accepted with sensible reservations, it is of great value in seeing the development of his work in an interesting way. The approach was first suggested in Russell Roth's essay in *Perspective* (Summer, 1949): "William Faulkner: The Pattern of Pilgrimage." I have chosen to elaborate upon Roth's terms because many qualifications of them are necessary to a full application of them.

I should like to think of the growth of Faulkner's work in terms of "central intelligences." This term has something in common with Henry James's use of it, though there are also many basic differences between his and Faulkner's use of the characters considered under it. Nor do I believe one can accept the term as meaning a character who in a given work "expresses the author's point of view." Faulkner does not *express* his point of view in this way. Nevertheless, at each of several stages of his career, he seems to be struggling toward the articulation of a human truth *in terms of* the disposition of one or another of his characters toward it. In other words, he at one and the same time *dramatizes* the truth; that is, a character in a given situation is affected by it and affects it and—through his own "voice"—gives it a value, a color, a quality that are a kind of auctorial interpretation of what is going on. Often this is merely a matter of style—of enforcing the rhetoric beyond the limits of a character's power of expression.[18]

The bald statement of the three classes of "central intelligence" requires much elaboration. They are (1) the "young esthete" (Roth's term for it as well); (2) the "good weak man"; and (3) the "good strong man." The esthete is so overcome by his view of evil that he is really beyond the point of even initiating any effective action with respect to it. He is Faulkner's version of a very special kind of Hamlet. He sees the evil entirely within himself, as though he were meditating endlessly before a mirror. He "gives up" acting, in any meaningful sense because he never gets beyond the psychological trap of introspection. Suicide is of course a primary recourse. If we can imagine Hamlet's committing suicide in the belief that he would thereby save the family honor, we might have a fairly clear vision of the "young esthete" as a defeating intelligence. This suggestion should, of course, lead one into a significant area of studies in modern literature, if the length and subject of this book permitted: the development, from Jules Laforgue's Hamlet to Eliot's "Prufrock" and eventually to the rich variety of "marginal sensitivities" that characterizes modern "heroism." Suffice it to say that—beginning in the postwar atmosphere of clever despair and disparagement—Faulkner also considered the frailties and inadequacies of this marginal personality.

Gradually, the Faulkner hero moved away from this point of almost absolute paralysis to the opposite position of archetypal "savior," or to the role of dramatizing virtues within an elaborate secular metaphor of human values. But Faulkner.

does not go all the way. His extraordinary skill as a narrative artist almost always combines with his practical recognition of human imperfections. When his hero seems to be moving toward the point of saintliness—to somewhere this side of the incredible role of man's usurping one or another of the privileges of God—he pulls him back. Nevertheless, Faulkner seemed—and especially in the work after 1950—to respond to pressures of moral enforcement. He wanted to prove man positively, actively, articulately virtuous; and his heroes became more and more clamorously and obviously Yoknapatawpha versions of either one or the other of the biblical Testaments.

Of course, throughout Faulkner's work a leavening process is going on. Average courage and faith and endurance are expressed by quite ordinary persons. "Decency" prevails often when extremes of either good or evil seem to have taken over. There is the quite simple heroism of "a good day's work done well"; and, on occasion—as in *Intruder, The Unvanquished,* and the final section of *The Sound and the Fury*—the quiet heroism of the ordinary person seems to prevail. In addition, Faulkner provides fine brief insights into life which seem to be in the nature of an aside spoken by a minor character before the curtain descends upon major action. The Negro Job, for example, speaks the general view of Jason Compson and thus puts him in the line of our own observation of him:

> "You's too smart for me. Aint a man in dis town kin keep
> up wid you for smartness. You fools a man what so smart he
> cant even keep up wid hisself," he says, getting in the wagon
> and unwrapping the reins.
> "Who's that?" I says.
> "Dat's Mr. Jason Compson," he says.
> "Git up dar, Dan!" (*SF*, 267).

Quentin Compson puts the matter effectively in another of these brief and tentative insights. Speaking of the place of Negroes in a white Southerner's life, he muses:

> . . . They come into white people's lives like that in sudden
> sharp black trickles that isolate white facts for an instant in

unarguable truth like under a microscope; the rest of the
time just voices that laugh when you see nothing to laugh
at, tears when no reason for tears . . . (*SF*, 189).

The "young esthete" appears at the very beginning of Faulkner's career. He is at first, though only briefly, a returned
soldier: Mahon of *Soldiers' Pay* is, however, too much the
victim of the war to be an intelligence of any sort; and his
position has to be articulated by others. The real value of the
novel comes from the contrast and conflict of responses to his
horrifying condition and his move toward death. A better example of the "young esthete" returned from the wars is the
young Bayard Sartoris. He is truly the young man who is
unable to cope, not only with society at large, but with his
own role as victim of its chaos. As Irving Howe has said,
Bayard "cannot reach a level of awareness that will bring
him self-knowledge; his intelligence is unequal to his despair"
(29). But this phase of the "young esthete" as a central intelligence concludes with Quentin Compson. His gestures of
"heroism" are all stimulated by himself and are never checked
against the reality of the external world. His role is entirely
"literary," allusive, intellectually isolated and abstract; he is
an example of what Henry James called the "closed self,"
but he is also quite unlike the Jamesian hero for he is a romantically self-indulgent person. He *thinks* of acting heroically
for a "cause," but the cause is absorbed, assimilated, vitiated
by his ego. His suicide is, therefore, *not* heroic because the
cause is never successfully projected beyond self.

None of these characters actually "speaks for" Faulkner;
nor does Faulkner speak for them. Faulkner's actual involvement in his characters, as distinguished from their being objective dramatizations, is difficult to determine. Quentin is
hero only in being most intensely disturbed by the defection
of his sister; what he feels and what he does are not admirable,
and Faulkner does not present him as heroic; but he does
offer an extended discussion of his failure in the concluding
pages of Part Two of *The Sound and the Fury*.

The ambiguities of the Faulkner hero's attempts to act in re-

lation to the evil and chaos in society are more vividly presented in the second group of heroes–the "good weak hero."
He is "good" because he *intends* to act positively and with
merit; but his weaknesses, whatever they are, quite definitely
prevent his success in having a moral effect. The first clear
example is Horace Benbow of *Sartoris* and *Sanctuary*. Benbow
fails to do good because his vision of evil destroys his will (he
returns from the Memphis brothel overwhelmed by an evil
he cannot really understand) and because of inner weaknesses
in the ordinary "man of good will." Benbow cannot rescue
either Temple Drake or Lee Goodwin from their fates, and
he is finally in serious danger of being himself trapped by the
evil he is fighting. It is significant that, when in *Requiem for a
Nun* Faulkner decided to review the subject of *Sanctuary*,
Benbow disappeared altogether from it and was replaced by
Gavin Stevens, his primary candidate for the role of "good
strong hero."

A much more persuasive example of the "good weak hero"
is Ratliff of *The Hamlet* and subsequent novels. Ratliff is an
eminently rational man. He is, moreover, a man of great humor
and emotional flexibility. We may say also that he is a man of
wisdom: he is able to translate the often comically irrational
behavior of Frenchman's Bend's ordinary citizens into folk
wisdom. He is also shrewd, clever, interested in the complications of the "deal" and the "swap." In *The Hamlet* the rational man is given a position of importance for the first time
in Faulkner's fiction.[19] But he does not prevail; he is still the
"weak" man because he cannot go all the way in leadership,
and the irrational desires of his fellow men are too powerful
and too insistent for him to prevail against them. More than
that, he is a man of sympathy, of emotional power, and this
tendency to give in to moods of anger and of horror proves
him to be unequal to Flem Snopes's absolutely unemotional
shrewdness. In the end Ratliff is also proved to be gullible:
he does not want easy money, but he can't resist the excitement and adventure of trying for it, and in the end he is just
one more victim of Snopes's superbly described treachery.

In many ways Ratliff is the best balanced and the most credible of all of Faulkner's "good" characters; his defeat at the end of *The Hamlet* does not mean that he has lost all sense of balance and is mad—like Henry Armstid—because of the force of his obsession. He continues, in *The Town* and *The Mansion,* to act and talk in conformity with the stance of the earlier novel, and he joins Gavin Stevens and Chick Mallison in the last two novels as men who have not only good will but occasionally the strength to implement it.

The "good strong man" is almost entirely a product of Faulkner's late sensitivity to human wrong and to his power to prevail beyond it. In an interview with Cynthia Grenier (*Accent*, 1956), he said "There isn't any theme in my work, or maybe if there is, you can call it a certain faith in man and his ability to always prevail and endure over circumstances and over his own destiny." This view has its own risks, and the real danger is that Faulkner will sacrifice characterization to conviction. All of his heroes who belong in this third group run this risk. His pre-eminent heroic "spokesman" is Gavin Stevens, whom one critic, overcome by the euphoria of Faulkner's Nobel speech assertions, called "a personification of the regenerated South."[20]

Stevens is by no means uniformly presented in a favorable sense. For one thing, he talks too much and is often in a position of Auden's captain, "Lecturing on navigation while the ship is going down." Just where does Faulkner stand with respect to Stevens's oratory and rhetoric? He obviously admires many of his ideas, but feels often that to make him simply a man of wisdom would be to give up all pretense to characterization. So he has Stevens default in the responsibilities of action in *Intruder,* and the real heroism of that novel is that of the young boy Chick Mallison, his Negro friend Aleck Saunder, and the old lady Miss Habersham. On other occasions, Stevens becomes what appears to be the dedicated moral "saint." In *Requiem for a Nun,* for example, he is a lawyer only superficially; and he resembles Benbow of *Sanctuary* only in this professional sense. His actual role is that of a secular father confessor, who must convince Temple Drake of her complicity in evil.

In many respects, the conception of a good strong hero goes so far toward pure moral abstraction that it yields eventually in *A Fable* to a mixture of allegory and fable. In this novel the figure of the hero loses all personal substance. The corporal *is* a person who acts out his mission, but his acts are never free of Faulkner's purpose. *A Fable* is not fiction in the sense we are accustomed to knowing it, but a "morality" in which literature is always subordinate to transcendent principle and message.[21]

Obviously Faulkner is puzzled over what he should do to enforce his assertions and still remain an artist. In his early fiction the moral truths were also there, but they were implicit; that is, they were acted out and dramatically contained. In fact, any too overt or too persistent expression of them was considered in "bad taste," in the sense of being a violation of balance and an abnormal extension of human possibility. Stevens, however, turns what is either comedy or pathos in the early fiction into a sententiously serious pose; and the corporal of *A Fable* is translated beyond the understanding of man. But this exaggeration does not mean that Faulkner has abandoned his interest in human variety. *The Mansion* in many respects restores his fiction to the artful balancing of extremes characteristic of his earlier work.[22]

The scope of Faulkner's work can now be seen from several vantage points. It is necessary to appreciate both its range and the value of its individual achievement. Faulkner's novels, as seen from the large perspective, are closely interrelated. This sense of relevance from one novel to another comes partly from the narrow concentration upon Yoknapatawpha County, which yields variety as well as cross-resemblances. Characters move from novel to novel; details of landscape are repeated; and though Faulkner shifts from place to place and from class to class of people, the lie of the land is the same from novel to novel.[23] Despite his latter-day temptation to make truth a fixed and irrevocable thing, Faulkner's works contain a succession of explorations of the varying and shifting nature of truth, as it is seen from many different human perspectives. Another way of seeing the novels is, therefore, as experiments in style and structure not only with human situations but also with the "eternal verities" he spoke of in the Stockholm address.

CHAPTER 2

Some Beginnings

I

SOLDIERS' PAY and *Mosquitoes* are the work of a man finding his way. They are both, in one way or another, the product of six months spent in New Orleans in 1925, some of the time in the company of Sherwood Anderson. They were not in any real sense indebted to Anderson as a master of style, though *Mosquitoes* echoes him in several respects. The novels are interesting primarily as the expressions of a man of talent who has not yet found either his proper form or subject.[1]

Soldiers' Pay is in the spirit of the postwar novel of the 1920's. Hero Donald Mahon returns from the War to his home in Charlestown, Georgia, horribly wounded, blinded, and dying. The "truth" of his condition is the focus of all the novel's portrayals; each character identifies himself in terms of his reaction to this specimen of what the French called (in the title of their translation) *Monnaie de Singe*. These persons include his father, an Episcopal clergyman; Cecily Saunders, his fiancée, who is thrown off balance by Mahon's unexpected return; two persons who have accompanied "the body" to Georgia, Margaret Powers, a young war widow, and Joe Gilligan, an enlisted man. As though emerging from a Swinburnian wood, the figure of Januarius Jones gives the novel the quality of a quite un-Faulknerian Pan and satyr.

The atmosphere of pseudo-Eliotic and postwar "disillusion" is pervasive, as it is in *Mosquitoes;* and his attempts to imitate a mood without knowing its supporting details accurately are all but disastrous. Jones's philandering pursuits of fleeing females contrast strangely with the somber bitterness of Donald Mahon's lingering death. Jones is, of course, supposed to typify the facetious remoteness of civilian life from the horror that was Mahon's war. The shock of Mahon's appearance ruins the sweetly superficial poise of Cecily Saunders; and Jones's leering "courtship" of her completes her ruin as a credible person.

Faulkner's intention is to portray each of these persons as isolated, whether from fear or obscene indifference, from any meaningful center of familial or social vitality. In the one case, Mahon is a victim of the war's violence, who, unseeing and almost insentient, is moving toward his death. The scar of his wound stands as a ghastly barrier to all vitality and defeats emotional sympathy. At the other extreme is Januarius Jones, who is also isolated from humanity but from his own choice in a 1920 revival of 1890 nonchalance. Both Mahon and Jones are indifferent; and the indifference is not conspicuously dissimilar in its effect. In a real sense Mahon's is, however, the more damaging because more disastrously the result of an unwilled calamity.

All of these rather carefully balanced figures of isolation and distress are an expression of postwar disillusion; but they are a quite artificial imitation of what his contemporaries were doing. Cecily Saunders is likewise an imitation of the flapper of F. Scott Fitzgerald; but she is treated with a satirical harshness far beyond Fitzgerald's power. Cecily's engagement to Mahon had originally been like Daisy Fay's to Gatsby of *The Great Gatsby*: the romance and glamor of the soldier's promise had captivated her. But his return marks both the end of all human romance and the depths of her selfishness. In spite of this obvious rebuke, one cannot really accept her triviality because no one is realized in the novel; they are all only seen as victims of vague terror and helplessness. It is a kind of impasse typical of those encountered by Aldous Huxley's characters in the 1920's novels.

Only the clergyman father of the hero seems to retain balance and to see beyond the center of aimless horror. He has a "philosophy" which enables him to survive, a point of view which—if one wishes to push hard at the absolute "unity" of Faulkner's work—emphasizes particularly an acceptance of the inevitability of evil, both human and nonhuman. The rector's faith is firmly grounded in an acceptance which is vaguely similar to the endurance and basic integrity of Dilsey.

In a backward view of *Soldiers' Pay*, gained from much and long attention to the major works, the balancing of types of isolation and of human fallibilities marks a beginning experiment in the neat, brilliant explorations of truth and individual perspectives of Faulkner's later work. Especially relevant are the elder Mahon's respect for inevitable death, disease, and violence, his having considered these within the human economy, and the suggestive allusions to religion. But in *Soldiers' Pay*, the representation is imperfect; it is troubled by the weaknesses of a young writer trying to find his style through lend and lease, and by his distortion of characters to make them typical of borrowed and imperfectly realized attitudes.

Mosquitoes is even less successful. In this avowed imitation of Aldous Huxley, Faulkner tried to do what Huxley did with a number of half-comical and cynical types in his early novels. But Faulkner accomplishes something in even a third-rate attempt, if it is only to suggest themes and rhetoric of the later work. Briefly, *Mosquitoes* describes a yachting party off New Orleans. The guests, assembled by a Mrs. Maurier, a wealthy widow, with the assistance of a teen-age niece, are an ill-assorted group: some artists and writers from the French bohemian quarter, an Englishman, a department-store buyer, and several others. In the course of the excursion, the niece elopes with the steward, is mercilessly attacked by mosquitoes in a nearby swamp, and is forced to return to the yacht. Since this is almost all of the "action" of the novel, it must rely for its effects upon talk about "ideas," attitudes, and contemporary mores. These Faulkner had picked up in his postwar years of reading and observing, but he is not skillful in relatively cheap repartee. The ideas do not communicate especially well, and such serious exponents of them as Gordon, the sculptor, are incapable of sustaining them as much more than poses. Gordon is obviously intended by Faulkner as a "heavyweight," but he comes perilously close to being a stereotyped figure.

Of course, we may regard *Mosquitoes* another way but obviously not the way Faulkner intended in 1927: that is, to see it as an examination of the failure of language to realize truth. As Olga Vickery has indicated, this view is not inconsistent with Faulkner's elaborate explorations of language and experience in the later novels:

> . . . Here, as in the later novels, truth is dependent not on words but on a moment of comprehension which usually occurs when the individual is least concerned with intellectual activity. . . .[2]

Such a view of *Mosquitoes*, of course, puts a quite different perspective upon the aimless and not very intelligent discussions in it. Their failures become the proof of a thesis rather than of their ineptitude and insubstantiality. The basic separation of words and deeds, in itself a part of the Huxley kind of satire of the 1920's, is in this sense a more fundamental issue; it is, as we shall see, to have a major role in such novels as *The Sound and the Fury* and *As I Lay Dying*. Mrs. Vickery points out (*Novels*, 9) that the persons who impress most with the genuineness of their achievement are least interested in talk, and *vice versa;* and the novelist-character of *Mosquitoes*, Fairchild, is appropriately embarrassed over the "sterility" of words as substitutes for actions:

> "You begin to substitute words for things and deeds, like the withered cuckold husband that took the Decameron to bed with him every night, and pretty soon the thing or the deed becomes just a kind of shadow of a certain sound you make by shaping your mouth a.certain way, . . ."[3]

This statement (qualified later when Fairchild defends his craft) is certainly a means of emphasizing the difference between words and deeds; but it would be a mistake to take this as a brilliant idea brilliantly executed. It is, after all, in the context of this very weak novel a commonplace that has been more effectively presented by scores of writers in the history of literature. Only in the light of its much more effective development in later fiction can it be considered important. Statement is one thing; and, if that is all a novel has, or almost all, the quality of the statement is of the essence. This it definitely does not have in *Mosquitoes*. Faulkner does set "being" against "saying," as Mrs. Vickery points out, but *Mosquitoes* does not emphasize the conflict in any significant way; we are left with a static novel, imperfectly supported by talk that is often inane and never decisive.

All of the work before 1929 seems to show Faulkner without a clear purpose and unaware either of what he wanted to say or of how he should say it. The style of his first two novels is often luxuriant without aim, flat when it should be crucially emphatic, trite and unoriginal. That later novels should prove to have followed ways suggested here testifies more to Faulkner's persistence than to the genius of his early years. The truth is that he was an indifferent writer until (in the novels beginning in 1929) he settled upon what he called his "postage stamp of native soil." The two novels published in 1929, *Sartoris* and *The Sound and the Fury*, show that he had "arrived" scarcely before he had troubled to travel there. It was as though the myth and legend and fable were at hand ready for him to tap at will. This is not altogether true. *Sartoris* is in some sense a transitional work; in it, the first World War was brought into relief in terms of the Civil War, and the exhaustive examination of violence and the past's burden began. Besides its being a study of Yoknapatawpha, *The Sound and the Fury* is the greatest American example of the stream-of-consciousness novel.

Sartoris is also a beginning of Faulkner's use of family tradition. Like the Compsons, the Sartorises are an established family, whose newer generation is bewildered and weakened by moral and intellectual confusions. But Faulkner is trying no easy postwar formula of "sterility and futility." While echoes of Eliot persist in Faulkner's work to testify that he had also served an apprenticeship, the full weight of his original talent soon proves too much for a slender imitative line. For all that, *Sartoris* is not yet equal to Faulkner's best, which was immediately to follow it. As Robert Cantwell has said,

> The dividing line in his work between its arty and frivolous earlier phase, and the power of its great period, is in *Sartoris*. More specifically, it is in something in *Sartoris* that reached beyond the novel itself and gave Faulkner the vision of his work as a whole. . . . Turning from [his first two novels] to *Sartoris* we find ourselves at once in the concrete reality of the town of Jefferson, seventy-five miles from Memphis, a town in upland country, lying in tilted slopes against the unbroken blue of the hills, in the midst of good broad fields richly somnolent. . . .[4]

The young Bayard Sartoris is a returned aviator, like Donald Mahon of *Soldiers' Pay;* and he is in spirit otherwise associated with the other novel. As William Van O'Connor describes him in *Tangled Fire* (33), he is "an offspring of the world-weary young men in the *fin de siècle* tradition." He is maddened by the memory of his brother's death in an air fight of the war, and he risks his life in dare-devil exploits. He deliberately courts death and wins her in the last of a series of test flights. The young Bayard is a man of compulsive violence. He poses a problem Mahon was incapable of suggesting: he goes forth actively to create the circumstances of violence, instead of permitting them to trap him, in a spirit of meaningless but not unmotivated heroism.

The essential difference between *Sartoris* and *Soldiers' Pay* lies in the frame of reference the later novel has. If the young Bayard cannot penetrate to the larger meaning of his acts, Faulkner can and does. Heroism is the subject of *Sartoris*. The blind anger and fear of the young man are a recurrence of the passion of inspired risk in the past. Faulkner is here so much better than he had been, because he is no longer writing in a vacuum. It is not at all that he needed something to be "romantic" about, but that he needed a structure of past and present, action and motive, within which to measure the value of human acts. He is not good at defining these acts unless they are put within such a frame, whether of a complex society or of a tradition or of both. His humor serves him well, and—as in other novels—aging women and Negroes cast skeptical doubts upon romantic pretension and excessive rhetoric. *Sartoris* is, therefore, a better novel than any he had previously written because it is richer in details and firmer in its judgment of their cultural context.

The young Bayard is only superficially the subject of the novel; it concerns not him but his relationship to four generations of Sartorises, comprehending both Civil War and World War I. The significance of past is here fully documented. Bayard must reconcile himself, not only to the violence of his war, but to its sources in history. When his reaction to his war is seen in its shocking and excessive way, it is both an inheritance from and a check upon the legend emerging from the past.

This novel is the beginning of Faulkner's analysis of the legend. His Yoknapatawpha people are often aware of it and of its consequences; they brood over its meaning, they assume its apparent burdens, they share the reactions to its now dimly seen or remembered character. Bayard Sartoris's experience helps to bring the legend within range of reality; the legend recedes, the reality explodes. But not quite: while Faulkner does not want to suggest a "romantic superiority" in the Civil War, there is a vital difference between the two wars in terms of degree and depth of commitment and impact. The violence of World War I is immediate, raw, and unalleviated; that of the Civil War has been subject to hundreds of redefinitions and has softened and even become glamorous in the process.

Here again Faulkner is concerned with examining perspectives upon the truth. Bayard Sartoris cannot bring himself to accepting violence of any sort as romantic; he is frustrated beyond belief by his own experience, and his mad dash for annihilation is, therefore, a result of his having found the legend disastrously misleading. The contrast of past with present acts also in the matter of the Sartoris family. They too, like the Civil War, have existed through several generations of time, and have acquired a legend. Both legends converge upon the lonely, present figure of the young Bayard. He is a forlorn and unhappy—though an angry—testimony of the collapse of legends.

But this is still not all: he is not, like Donald Mahon, to have the full weight of symbolic "message." He is not merely pathetic, or not wholly pathetic. He is, after all, gauche and erratic; and his actions are often comically foolish. There is something, after all, that sustains the human condition despite and beyond modern violence, and contrary to legend. Both the intensity of Bayard's courting of violence and the strength of family and tradition are false. *Sartoris* somehow strikes the balance between their kinds of falsehood. Faulkner often presents this figure of the past pushing against the present, the agony of the present trying to adjust to the past. Bayard Sartoris goes to his death in a gesture of aberrant heroism, as Quentin Compson was to commit suicide to protect a "legend" entirely abstracted from fact of any kind. Between the two—a legend and the reductive fact—there are intervening and alleviating agencies.

Miss Jenny of *Sartoris* brings Bayard's errantry down to a sensible level. Within the context of his wild vindictiveness, something must give in if the present and the past are to be restored to some level of decent comprehension. Miss Jenny acknowledges the power and persuasion of legend. Because the Sartorises go back into the past of legend, she knows that they have inherited from it a way of limiting and controlling character. But she also knows how to distinguish the illusory from the real. She is like Miss Habersham of *Intruder*, who also demonstrates a "practical heroism," knows what to do and why it is done. And in the end Miss Jenny knows the difference between fustian and mortality; seeing the graves and the stones of old Bayard and of son John, she reflects upon what it is that forces humans into violent and erratic action, to earn their right to a legend:

> But she knew what it would be, what with the virus, the inspiration and example of that one which dominated them all, which gave the whole place, in which the weary people were supposed to be resting, an orotund solemnity having no more to do with mortality than the bindings of books have to do with their characters, and beneath which the headstones of the wives whom they had dragged into their arrogant orbits were, despite their pompous genealogical references, modest and effacing as the song of thrushes beneath the eyrie of an eagle.[5]

CHAPTER *3*

The Original Talent

I

FAULKNER has several times referred to *The Sound and the Fury* as the favorite among his novels: ". . . I must judge it on the basis of that one which caused me the most grief and anguish, as the mother loves the child who became the thief or murderer more than the one who became the priest" (*Three Decades*, 73). It was the most difficult of the novels to date, because the most ambitious. He tried to do several things in it: to narrate a continuous story, to experiment in forms of interior monologue, to represent four very different points of view with rich variety.

Faulkner described the experience of writing the novel, in his remarks to Jean Stein:

I wrote it five separate times, trying to tell the story, to rid myself of the dream which would continue to anguish me until I did. . . . It began with a mental picture. I didn't realize at the time it was symbolical. The picture was of the muddy seat of a little girl's drawers in a pear tree, where she could see through a window where her grandmother's funeral was taking place . . . I had already begun to tell the story through the eyes of the idiot child, since I felt that it would be more effective as told by someone capable only of knowing what happened, but not why. I saw that I had not told the story that time. I tried to tell it again, the same story through the eyes of another brother. That was still not it. I told it for the third time through the eyes of the third brother. That was still not it. I tried to gather the pieces together and fill in the gaps by making myself the spokesman. It was still not complete, not until fifteen years after the book was published, when I wrote as an appendix to another book the final effort to get the story told and off my mind, so that I myself could have some peace from it . . . (*Three Decades*, 73-74).[1]

These remarks at least suggest that the novel is constructed upon a successive retelling of a single story from four different points of view. The facts of the story are few and fairly easy to record: the earliest significant event, the death of the grandmother in 1898, thirty years in the past; Caddy's affair with Dalton Ames in 1909, the first of a series of affairs; her marriage to Herbert Head in April of 1910 and the subsequent birth of her illegitimate child, Miss Quentin, which causes the annulment of the marriage; the suicide of Quentin, June of 1910; the death of the father in 1913; and the elopement of Miss Quentin with the contents of Jason's money box, and Jason's futile effort to capture her, Easter Sunday of 1928.

These facts are told and retold four different times from entirely different perspectives. In the first three cases, we are within the minds of the three brothers—Benjy, Quentin, and Jason, in that order—and adjust to their perspective upon the story and upon the truth of it as each sees it. In Part Four, the perspective shifts from an interior monologue to a straightforward narrative; the point of view is Faulkner's but the "informing genius" of the section is Dilsey. The effect of this arrangement, once one has become used to it, is fascinating; and there is no denying its appropriateness.

Robert Humphrey has made this shrewd observation about both this novel and *As I Lay Dying*: Faulkner's "chief unifying device . . . is a unity of action. . . . In other words, he uses a substantial plot, the thing that is lacking in all other stream-of-consciousness literature. . . . It is the thing that carries *As I Lay Dying* and *The Sound and the Fury* away from the pure stream-of-consciousness novel to a point where the traditional novel and stream of consciousness are combined."[2] This is to say that the usual stream-of-consciousness novel is concerned with revealing the inner minds of its characters, but that movement and action are only incidentally revealed.

The Sound and the Fury does two things: it plays upon the consciousness of Benjy, Quentin, and Jason, representing them in style, syntax, and image as nearly accurately as is consistent with the demands of the other task; it tells, and retells, a specific story, which has a sequence and succession of events leading through thirty years of Compson history. These two tasks are advanced in each section with an ingenuity and skill that enrich the account and give it a variety of meanings no traditional narrative could have achieved.

This novel is no *tour de force*. It is not what early critics accused it of being: a masterpiece of creative chicanery, designed to confuse and outrage the reader.[3] "By fixing the structure while leaving the central situation ambiguous," Mrs. Vickery writes, "Faulkner forces the reader to reconstruct the story and to apprehend its significance for himself. . . ." In this sense, the novel is a problem in definition, in the meaning or the "truth" of any human situation, as it is seen in very different ways. Mrs. Vickery also suggests in *Novels* (29) that the theme of *The Sound and the Fury* is "the relation between the act and man's apprehension of the act, between the event and the interpretation." Faulkner's characters are involved, many of them deeply involved, in trying to define an event to themselves. In this case at least, we are asked to become involved with them, since the only way the style will make sense to us is to have us look at events in the Compson family as each of the brothers sees them, in the act of their happening and in retrospect.

The central event of *The Sound and the Fury* is Candace's (Caddy's) affair with Dalton Ames. It is her "sin," her breach of ethics or contract, her act of bringing the outside world within the Compson family pattern. It is seen "out of proportion" in each of the first three sections; it is re-examined in part four and there seen as far less important than it had been earlier. Faulkner gives us both an inner and an outer view of it. He moves from one kind of subjective view to another, finally into the world itself, so that we may gaze at the place and the site of its happening. Truth would seem, therefore, to be a matter of perspective; we are aware not so much of truth itself but of a version of the truth, a distortion of it, which must be set right, and eventually is. Above all, Faulkner is saying that any truth is far more complex than it appears on the surface to be.

As we already know, Faulkner spoke in his interview with Mrs. Stein of "the picture . . . of the muddy seat of a little girl's drawers . . ." (*Three Decades*, 73). The incident occurs in 1898; Caddy, playing with her brothers in the "branch," falls into the mud and stains her drawers. In the evening Dilsey tries to rub out the stain, but doesn't succeed: "Just look at you," she says, "It done soaked clean through onto you." (*SF*, 93) The stain becomes the sin of her affairs, leading to Miss Quentin, the illegitimate child; and in the end the image of the mud stain is replaced "by the one of the fatherless and motherless girl climbing down the rainpipe to escape from the only home she had, where she had never been offered love or affection or understanding" (*Three Decades*, 73). The first three sections of the novel are concerned with the three distinct views of Caddy's "stain." Caddy means something different in each case; Mrs. Vickery has described it in *Novels* (30): "For Benjy she is the smell of trees; for Quentin, honor; and for Jason, money or at least the means of obtaining it." In part four, Caddy all but disappears, though her role in Jason's conflict with Miss Quentin is quite clearly in the background.

Faulkner adjusts the style, the imagery, and the narrative sequence of each of the sections to the point of view from which it is being written. Benjy's world is a fixed one, a world of sensations, one without time: all of these characteristics come from the fact that he is a thirty-three-year-old idiot who stopped growing mentally in 1898 at the age of three. He cannot abstract or generalize, cannot distinguish between one time and another, and can only react to a number of fixed sensory conditions that repeat themselves to him again and again. Here memory and sense are inseparable: a thirty-year difference in time is no difference at all, and sensations that are actually separated by twenty or thirty years are undifferentiated.

These characteristics explain the curious kind of fixed world we inhabit in section one; they also explain Benjy's instinctive reactions to any disturbance of that world. For example, Caddy when she is "right" to Benjy "smells like trees"; when she doesn't smell like trees, something has gone wrong; and Benjy sets up a howl of protest, his only way of registering a complaint or of passing a moral judgment. As in this case, when Caddy has been with "Charlie," one of a number of successors to Dalton Ames (the time is 1909):

> Caddy and I ran. We ran up the kitchen steps, onto the porch, and Caddy knelt down in the dark and held me. I could hear her and feel her chest. "I wont," she said. "I wont anymore, ever. Benjy. Benjy." Then she was crying, and I cried, and we held each other. "Hush," she said. "Hush. I wont anymore." So I hushed and Caddy got up and we went into the kitchen and turned the light on and Caddy took the kitchen soap and washed her mouth at the sink, hard. Caddy smelled like trees (*SF*, 67).

This detail is repeated many times, and Benjy's response to Caddy's departure from the Compson place in 1912 is sensed as a lack, an absence, which is compensated for by the sound of "caddy" on the neighboring golf course and by the presence of Miss Quentin, who becomes like her mother in many respects in Benjy's mind. The absolute limitations of Benjy's power to discriminate one thing from another, and one time from another, mean that we are in a fixed world outside of time and change. Benjy does not want change; it upsets him. He is quite incapable of seeing Caddy as a person who will change, grow old and exist in time. In a sense Benjy wants a simple world (the world more or less fixed for him when he was three) that does not change and is above and beyond the effects of passing time.

The strategy of placing Benjy's section at the beginning yields dividends: our first encounter with the Compson family is in terms of childhood (almost, of childlike innocence); it is a simple world, from which all decline and decay and breakdown are to begin. As we encounter family events later in the novel, we do so with the memory of Benjy's original and "pure" response to them. Finally, Benjy's non-abstract, overly simple "moral sense" is reduced to a number of minimal responses: he senses, smells evil, and passes an instinctive judgment upon elementary disruptions of a fixed world.

The Benjy section closes with a series of quick alternations of farthest past and immediate present—the present of Easter Saturday, April 7, 1928, Benjy's birthday. As Benjy undresses in 1928, he watches Miss Quentin escape down the pear tree outside their rooms (the two trees, of 1898 and 1928, fuse, as do the two persons): ". . . We went to the window and looked out. It came out of Quentin's window and climbed across into the tree. We watched the tree shaking. The shaking went down the tree, then it came out and we watched it go away across the grass . . ." (*SF*, 92-93).[4]

For all its greater complexity, the second or Quentin's section also presents a fixed world which he is desperately trying to preserve—but for his own reasons. One notices immediately the difference of language, the variety of figures and allusions, the appeals to undergraduate erudition, the forms of "debate" going on in his mind along rhetorical lines. Yet Quentin sees Caddy in much the same way as Benjy: in giving herself to Dalton Ames, she has violated a world that has before this been fixed; she has gone outside an established place and time, has set time and growth and decay going. Quentin also protests, in his own way, as violently and as vigorously as Benjy.

In his appendix to the *Portable Faulkner* (the "fifth attempt" to write the story), Faulkner speaks of Quentin as the person "who loved not his sister's body but some concept of Compson honor precariously and (he knew well) supported by the minute fragile membrane of her maidenhead as a miniature replica as all the whole vast globy earth may be poised on the nose of a trained seal . . ." (*SF*, 9). Quentin's mission is to save the Compson "honor" by arresting time and thus forcing decay out of the Compson world. He is in love with stasis, represented variously by the *place* of the Compson home, by Caddy's virginity, and eventually by death itself.

Quentin's great and powerful enemy is time—clock and calendar time—and he fights it throughout his day of June 2, 1910. Mrs. Vickery describes his world in *Novels* (37) as "an ethical order based on words, on 'fine, dead sounds,' the meaning of which he has yet to learn. He has, in short, separated ethics from the total context of humanity." In his own way, Faulkner has made this difference between words and humanity one of his major themes throughout his work. Similarly, Quentin demands that Caddy remain "outside of time," but she is in time and cannot break from it; she is a time creature and will therefore of necessity violate both Benjy's percept and Quentin's concept of a fixed world.

Quentin sets himself the role of guardian of the Compson honor. Within the design of what he assumes it to be, he tries to set up his own system of rewards and punishments, of good and evil. Quentin is aware, on this day at Harvard, of the relentless move of time from light to darkness, from his life to his death. Clocks and watches tell the time, and he desperately tries to prove them wrong or unreliable. His body casts a shadow, as does his life as it moves within the years of family history; he tries to stamp out the shadow, and eventually succeeds with his suicide. But the shadow is just one of the reminders of the natural order: the odor of the honeysuckle takes him back to Mississippi, to Caddy's wedding to Herbert Head, and to the unavoidable facts of time and change. The honeysuckle is a sexual reminder, a reminder of rank luxuriant growth and decay, signalized in Caddy's illicit affairs. When the "paradise" of his childhood world fails, he tries to convert Caddy's sin into incest, to contain it within a fixed world he can control. He will change a paradise into hell, so that it be his own: *"Only you and me then amid the pointing and the horror walled by the clean flame"*[5] (*SF*, 136). As George M. O'Donnell has said, he is trying to "transform meaningless degeneracy into significant doom" (*Three Decades*, 86).

Quentin's efforts are not merely causeless quixoticism. His monologue reveals again and again the failure of the Compson family to hold together. This passage, for example, from his memory of Caddy's wedding in April, 1910 suggests a number of themes that converge upon Quentin's final act:

> There was no nigger in this street car, and the hats unbleached as yet flowing past under the window. Going to Harvard. [the street car, but also Quentin of a year before] We have sold Benjy's [the pasture land sold by the Compsons to a golf club, to provide the money for Quentin's Harvard year] *He lay on the ground under the window, bellowing.* [Benjy, on the occasion of Caddy's wedding] *we have sold Benjy's pasture so that Quentin may go to Harvard* a brother to you. Your little brother.

These last phrases are spoken by Mrs. Compson, and the time shift from June 2 at Harvard to April 22, 1910, in Jefferson, has been achieved.[5a]

> You should have a car [Herbert Head speaking] it's done you no end of good dont you think so Quentin I call him Quentin at once you see I have heard so much about him from Candace.

In the paragraph following, Mrs. Compson's remarks bring on a flow of tortured memory, of Quentin's attempts to wipe out Caddy's sin by claiming it as incest, and it ends with a complaint of his mother's total inadequacy:

> Why shouldn't you I want my boys to be more than friends yes Candace and Quentin more than friends *Father I have committed* [Quentin to his father, but an echo of the prayer of confession, showing Quentin's appropriation of religion to his own moral world] what a pity you had no brother or sister [his mother, to Herbert Head] *No sister no sister had no sister* Dont ask Quentin he and Mr. Compson both feel a little insulted when I am strong enough to come down to the table I am going on nerve I'll pay for it after it's all over and you have taken my little daughter away from me *My little sister had no. If I could say Mother. Mother* (SF, 113-14).

Quentin's section concludes with a brilliantly represented debate with the memory of his father's words. As he prepares to go to his suicide by drowning (for which he has been preparing throughout the day), echoes haunt him of what his father has said throughout his struggle against the knowledge of Caddy's sin. The dignity of his act, as he sees it, is questioned by his father until it, as well as Quentin's belief in it as an heroic sacrifice, is lost altogether.

> . . . and he we must stay awake and see evil done for a little while its not always and i it doesn't have to be even that long for a man of courage and he do you consider that courage and i yes sir dont you and he every man is the arbiter of his own virtues whether or not you consider it courageous is of more importance than the act itself . . . you are still blind to what is in yourself to that part of general truth the sequence of natural events and their causes which shadows every mans brow even benjys you are not thinking about finitude you are contemplating an apotheosis in which a temporary state of mind will become symmetrical above the flesh and aware both of itself and of the flesh . . . (195-96).

Jason's section, the third one, begins in a matter-of-fact "rational" way: "Once a bitch always a bitch, what I say" (198). In the Compson family appendix, Faulkner calls him "the first sane Compson since before Culloden and (a childless bachelor) hence the last. Logical rational contained and even a philosopher in the old stoic tradition: Thinking nothing whatever of God one way or another and simply considering the police and so fearing and respecting only the Negro woman [Dilsey] . . ." (16). This statement is of course an ironic tribute to Jason's reasonableness; it is like the "integrity" of Flem Snopes: limited, selfish, and inhumane.[6] To Jason, Caddy's sin simply means that because of it he has lost the bank job promised him by Herbert Head before the annulment of the marriage. He is out therefore to be recompensed for "breach of contract," withholds the checks sent by Caddy to support Miss Quentin, and saves the money in his locked tin box (which Miss Quentin rifles of its contents before she escapes).

These are the simple facts of Jason's consciousness. Without subtlety and rhetorical finish, it is racy and self-indulgent, bristling with spiteful innuendoes, withal "objective" and superficially graced with "common sense." Praised by his querulous mother as the only "sensible" Compson, he falls victim in the end to a kind of "legal illegal" irony, for in stealing his money Miss Quentin is not only getting her own back but also acting in the manner and spirit of Jason himself. So smart a man, as the Negro Job has said, can be outsmarted only by himself. Having cut off humanity, he is eventually defeated by it in the person of the "man with the red tie" (who is never otherwise specified) who runs off with Miss Quentin, and by a series of irrational disasters on his trip to recover his loot. Even to the end, however, he thinks of nothing but the "business deal" that has been revoked:

> . . . Of his niece he did not think at all, nor the arbitrary valuation of the money. Neither of them had had entity or individuality for him for ten years; together they merely symbolized the job in the bank of which he had been deprived before he ever got it (321).[7]

II

In section four we move, for the first time, into the world itself. We are still within the Compson family, but we are not involved within a Compson mind. We look quite dispassionately at the house from the outside—as though we had crossed the street for an appraising look. In this perspective it looks diminished and not a little grotesque, and certain revisions of perspective (which we had suspected were due) now take place. The first is the move of Dilsey to center, as the only fully balanced and genuine personality of the novel. Faulkner associates her dignity and power of endurance with universal truths and values, which will become the final means of judging Compsons. In the remarkable opening paragraphs, Dilsey is shown emerging from her quarters, dressed in Easter "finery":

The gown fell gauntly from her shoulders, across her fallen breasts, then tightened upon her paunch and fell again, ballooning a little above the nether garments which she would remove layer by layer as the spring accomplished and the warm days, in colour regal and moribund. She had been a big woman once but now her skeleton rose, draped loosely in unpadded skin that tightened again upon a paunch almost dropsical, as though muscle and tissue had been courage or fortitude which the days or the years had consumed until only the indomitable skeleton was left rising like a ruin or a landmark above the somnolent and impervious guts . . . (281-82).

We also become aware of what the others left in the Compson household look and sound like. Benjy looms before our eyes, "a big man who appeared to have been shaped of some substance whose particles would not or did not cohere to one another or to the frame which supported it . . ." (290). Jason and his mother appear together at the breakfast table, "the one cold and shrewd, with close-thatched hair curled into two stubborn locks, one on either side of his forehead like a bartender in caricature, and hazel eyes with black-ringed irises like marbles, the other cold and querulous, with perfectly white hair and eyes pouched and baffled and so dark as to appear to be all pupil or all iris" (295).

From these several objective portraits it becomes obvious that the one of Dilsey will dominate and that in its terms Faulkner intends a final perspective upon the Compson story. Mrs. Vickery says in *Novels* (47) that Dilsey represents "the ethical norm, the realizing and acting out of one's humanity; it is from this that the Compsons have deviated, each into his separate world. . . ." The perspective shifts not only to Dilsey but also to the Negro church, where the Easter Sunday services are to be heard. The major performer, the Reverend Shegog from Saint Louis, has a "wizened black face like a small, aged monkey" (309), but a powerful mission and message; it seemed that his body fed his voice to serve the mission. In his sermon about "the ricklickshun en de blood of de Lamb" (311), he turns to the simplicities of religious feeling, cutting through layers of Compson decay and reaching a universal level of judgment.

As Dilsey returns from the service, she mutters to herself: "I've seed de first en de last . . . I seed de beginnin, en now I sees de endin" (313). The beginning and the ending of the Compsons surely, since Jason will not contribute to another generation and Miss Quentin has fled from it. The house has collapsed, but its torture and its agony are finally put into a perspective not its own. *The Sound and the Fury* ends with the trip to the cemetery of Luster and Benjy. Luster mischievously turns the wrong corner; Jason, arriving just at the moment when Benjy bellows his protest against the derangement, violently sets the wagon straight; and it proceeds smoothly and serenely once more: "post and tree, window and doorway, and signboard, each in its ordered place" (336).

In the end, the novel is disposed of by the Negro servant and the idiot man. These serve to let us see the basic simplicities from which the Compson family has long since fled. We already know that Benjy's view is limited (he is a "Christ figure" only in a very limited sense[8]), that it has to be helped and ministered to constantly. This leaves us with Dilsey as "ethical norm." Nor should we take too seriously the suggestion that the Compson decline serves by analogy to represent the decline of Southern aristocracy.[9] The problems and responses within the novel are sufficient to the needs thereof. But, of course, they may lead to expansions beyond themselves—at whatever risk such expansions entail. Faulkner was himself to move outside and beyond the Compsons in *Absalom*, as we shall see.

III

As I Lay Dying superficially resembles *The Sound and the Fury* in being an experiment in interior monologue and narrative, in being a family story, and in setting the members of a family against each other. In the first case, *Dying* seems very much more difficult, but it is only more complicated. There are many more voices in the narration: some fifteen narrators, and fifty-nine divisions, instead of four. But these merely complicate and vary the action; for the movement is actually quite clear and more directly visualized (as well as smelled). In each of the fifty-nine passages, one Bundren or non-Bundren conducts the action along its way and, at the same time, reflects upon its meaning for him. These reflections are as varied as the degree of involvement in or commitment to the death and burial of the mother. A remarkable virtuosity of narrative-reflection results.

The action itself is simple: Addie Bundren dies; and, in answer to her wishes, the body is taken for burial to Jefferson, some forty miles away. But the weather intervenes, and flood waters require that the cortège take detours. Some nine days pass before the coffin, which before long clearly announces its passing to neighboring nostrils, is finally laid to rest. These days involve battling with flood water and a fire set by one of the children, the threat of buzzards, the hazards of a broken leg, and other incidental losses and disasters. In the end, after Addie is buried, her bereaved husband appears with the second Mrs. Bundren, "a kind of duck-shaped woman all dressed up, with them kind of hard-looking pop eyes like she was daring ere a man to say nothing."[10] She brings with her a gramophone as dowry, and the Bundren family is once more reunited (with the exception of Darl, who has been sent to the State Hospital at Jackson).

Faulkner has said that he decided "to expose the Bundren family to the two greatest disasters known to man: flood and fire."[11] But *Dying* is not merely a story of disasters or of a mission nobly achieved in spite of serious difficulties. Nor is it simply a comedy of horrors. Whatever it has of biblical or legendary suggestiveness is a matter of inference. Primarily, the novel is a psychological study of several perspectives upon a truth, and the truth in this case is not dying but the circumstances of being born and of living.

This interpretation of the novel makes Addie imperatively its center. It is her consciousness and her memory of the Bundren past that make the narrative passages of her family what they are: reflections in both style and point of view of the place of each Bundren in the whole. Addie has only one monologue to herself, but it is the key to the novel. It is ironically placed in the external action after her coffin has been rescued from flood waters by her son Jewel. The monologue occurs "as I lay dying," but it is revealed to us as she lay dead, her will still powerfully dictating the acts and temperaments of her children.

As the passage begins, Addie remembers her life as schoolmarm before her marriage to Anse: "I could just remember how my father used to say that the reason for living was to get ready to stay dead a long time . . ." (*Dying*, 461). To get away from the hateful school, she "took Anse"; and she shortly discovered, with the birth of their first child, that "living was terrible and that this was the answer to it. That was when I learned that words are no good; that words don't ever fit even what they are trying to say at . . ." (463). These "words" she remembers are Anse's, and Anse remains a "man of words," who shunts aside with words and folk pieties all responsibilities to act. But Cash, the first-born, who arrived before the dissolution of Addie's love and trust, proves a reliable, practical, and a sensible person—in a sense, the "folk hero" of the novel.

Cash's birth was the dividing line in Addie's relationship with her husband. She now knew "that we had had to use one another by words like spiders dangling by their mouths from a beam . . ." (463). A word was "just a shape to fill a lack" (464). But she is further embittered in the second birth: "Then I found that I had Darl. . . . It was as though [Anse] had tricked me, hidden within a word like within a paper screen and struck me in the back through it . . ." (464). Her bitterness over the "trick" is translated into hostility for Darl, who becomes the most vocal, the most strangely upset, and eventually the destructive member of the family. His acts and his words are both desperate stratagems to assert himself as a member of the human race and of a family. The rhetoric of Darl's words and the violence of his acts are a direct result of the circumstances of his birth.

At this point Addie fully realizes "how words go straight up in a thin line and how terribly doing goes along the earth, clinging to it, so that after a while the two lines are too far apart for the same person to straddle from one to the other . . ." (465). She severs all meaningful relationship with her husband ("And then he died. He did not know he was dead." 466); and she has an affair with the preacher, Whitfield, also a man of words. Jewel is the result, a bastard son.

The birth of Jewel is a consequence of her testing the word "sin" against the act of it. The act is vitiated because Whitfield does not deeply participate in it, but Jewel becomes to her the only real son, the only one not associated with Anse. "With Jewel . . . the wild blood boiled away and the sound of it ceased . . . and I lying calm in the slow silence, getting ready to clean my house" (467). To Jewel Addie entrusts her salvation—which is to mean the successful progress of her coffin to the family grave in Jefferson. Before she died, she had said to Cora Tull (an imperceptive and smugly righteous neighbor) that Jewel "is my cross and he will be my salvation. He will save me from the water and from the fire. Even though I have laid down my life, he will save me" (460).

Jewel does just this. He is a man of few words (only one monologue is given him, and it is full of hatred for the other Bundrens), and he believes in pure act. *Dying's* great dramatic conflict has nothing to do with Anse's "fulfilling his mission"—or is only incidentally concerned with it; it is essentially a novel of the tensions between Darl and Jewel, the one an unwanted and the other an illegitimate son. About the other children, Addie says, "I gave Anse Dewey Dell to negative Jewel. Then I gave him Vardaman to replace the child I had robbed him of. And now he has three children that are his and not mine. And then I could get ready to die" (467).

Addie's monologue is brilliantly explanatory. The peculiarities of the style and the strange shifts of action are dissolved in the light of Addie's control over her children's status and their response to it. It is fitting also that Vardaman and Dewey

Dell should come close in the end to Darl's position: They are all three children of Anse and only indifferently of Addie Vardaman's style of monologue even approaches Darl's, in spite of a disparity of some twenty years in their ages (Vardaman is about eight, Darl twenty-eight). Darl's curious power to see beyond space and time barriers is also explained; his speculation upon being is directly related to his sense of isolation from his mother:

> I don't know what I am. I don't know if I am or not. Jewel knows he is, because he does not know that he does not know whether he is or not . . . (396).

Jewel *is* in terms of Addie's being; when Addie dies and is finally buried, Jewel's *is* will become was. But Darl's existence depends on his breaking through that being; and when he fails, he fails altogether of being and goes off to the house of schizophrenics in Jackson, where the disparity of being and not-being will not matter. To this tragedy, the eminently sensible Cash offers some sensibly practical words:

> Sometimes I ain't so sho who's got ere a right to say when a man is crazy and when he ain't. Sometimes I think it ain't none of us pure crazy and ain't none of us pure sane until the balance of us talks him that-a-way . . . (510).

The affairs of the Bundrens are seen in the alternating bright glare and fitful light of their divergent consciousnesses. So far as they are concerned, their eccentricities are sufficiently explained. But these are imperfectly understood, if at all, by the non-Bundren world of some eight persons who divide sixteen passages. Of them, only Dr. Peabody seems to have a more than surface view of the Bundrens. In his one monologue, he speaks of death as "merely a function of the mind—and that of the ones who suffer the bereavement . . ." (368).[12] The other "outsiders" are variously dense, superficial, or quite charitably disposed. Their remarks turn the Bundren tension (which is at times comical enough) into surface comedy. And Cora Tull is one of Faulkner's finest comic figures. Her husband Vernon looks upon her "trust in my God and my reward" with a wry amusement: "I reckon if there's ere a man or woman anywhere that He could turn it all over to and go away with His mind at rest, it would be Cora. And I reckon she would make a few changes, no matter how He was running it. And I reckon they would be for man's good. Leastways, we would have to like them. Leastways, we might as well go on and make like we did" (391).

CHAPTER *4*

The Tangled Web

I

BEFORE COMPLETING the next two of his major works—
Light in August and *Absalom, Absalom!*—Faulkner wrote
what most people consider a "minor novel," *Sanctuary*. He
claims that he sat down in 1925 to write it as "a cheap idea,
. . . deliberately conceived to make money."[1] He tried to see
if he could write something that would sell at least ten thousand copies. When his publisher was shocked and returned
the manuscript to him, Faulkner revised it extensively.

Whatever the intention, the book was almost uniformly con-
demned when it appeared as "shocking," as "a calculated
assault on one's sense of the normal," as grimly stocked with
"sadistic cruelty," and as aimlessly "horrifying and morbid."[2]
Faulkner himself seems to have wanted to rescue the book
from its "base origins." He didn't, he said, have much control
of it once it had been in galley proofs: "It was in a way
already in the public domain."[3] But some of the facts and
some of the characters were rescued in a retrospective way
and re-examined in *Requiem for a Nun*. Nevertheless, *Sanctuary* has an important role in the Faulkner canon.

It is, for one thing, one of his most nearly exhaustive com-
mentaries, along the lines of a semi-*Waste Land* review, upon
modern society. The horror is not merely vindictive, nor is it
the result of Faulkner's exploitation of the sensational. The
novel is essentially an examination of the failure of the law—
of legal ethics, and of the moral strength of the "lawyer of

good will"—to account for or to fight against unmitigated evil. The two antagonists are Horace Benbow and Popeye, and each is superbly appropriate to his type. The contrast is seen immediately in the opening chapter when Benbow and Popeye confront each other before the spring: Benbow, "a tall, thin man, hatless, in worn gray flannel trousers and carrying a tweed coat over his arm. . ."; Popeye, with a face of "a queer, bloodless color, as though seen by electric light; against the sunny silence, in his slanted straw hat and his slightly akimbo arms, he had that vicious depthless quality of stamped tin" (*Sanctuary*, 1-2).

Popeye is an "unnatural creature." The images used to describe him are either metallic or mechanical. He hates and fears nature which is in every detail his antithesis. He dwells in a "gaunt ruin of a house," (20) about which "nowhere was any sign of husbandry—plow or tool; in no direction was a planted field in sight . . ." (47). Benbow, on the contrary, is a naive but well-intentioned man of good will and champion of the good and the just. "I cannot stand idly by and see injustice . . ." he tells his wife (141). There's a corruption about "even looking upon evil even by accident; you cannot haggle, traffic, with putrefaction . . ." (152). Yet he is unable really to cope with evil; experiencing it overcomes him; and the measured complications of the law are utterly inadequate for its irrational nature.

Benbow encounters evil in the case of Temple Drake, a co-ed who has accidentally wandered into the "jungle" of Popeye's country still. When he returns from Memphis and the sight of vicious impotence, Benbow is overcome:

> Better for her if she were dead tonight. . . . For me, too. He thought of her, Popeye, the woman, the child, Goodwin, all put into a single chamber, bare, lethal, immediate and profound: a single blotting instant between the indignation and the surprise. . . . Removed, cauterised out of the old and tragic flank of the world. . . . Perhaps it is upon the instant that we realise, admit, that there is a logical pattern to evil, that we die . . . (265-66).

This is a measure of his horror and of his defeat. Nevertheless, he persists in carrying on his errand of good will, impotently and unavailingly. He is incapable of sure, effective action for the good, and the failure of the law is halfway the failure of the lawyer. In the end, his effort to rescue Lee Goodwin from a murder charge that is clearly trumped up collapses in the irrational explosion of mob violence; Goodwin is lynched and Benbow narrowly escapes. But the failure is further complicated with Temple Drake's integrity and her failure in it, with her father's desire to save his reputation, and with the failure of the legal process and the legal expedient.

Evil is represented in *Sanctuary* as having a consistent, though a specious and a motiveless, logic of its own. Within its terms viciousness possesses an integrity, as Flem Snopes's acquisitiveness is wholly and consistently self-contained. What is lacking in each case (and in a dozen other cases in Faulkner's works) is a sense of humanity, a link to it, through either weakness or strength. And in his later works he tried to match evil of this kind with a sense of the right and the good that is as powerful as it and that has a chance to prevail over it.

Perhaps what distressed readers of *Sanctuary* more than its ingenious obscenities was the grinding helplessness of Benbow's good will. Faulkner was himself disposed to relinquish such futility; for the agonies of his later novels are allegorically or dramatically softened: a young boy, a Negro woman, or a bastard corporal steps in to endure evil and injustice, slowly and patiently to disprove it, or to prove that man can and will prevail over it. But *Sanctuary* is not so rescued. Benbow's weaknesses are almost sufficient to prove the triumph of evil over good; they are aided and abetted by Gowan Stevens's cowardice, by Temple Drake's corruption, by her father's anxiety to save face and reputation. In the end Popeye is himself a victim of "injustice"; he is executed for a crime he has not committed, and he does nothing to defend himself.[4]

II

In *Light in August* the problem of evil is much more intricately treated. It is viewed from every conceivable angle of vision, involvement, detachment, inner necessity and outer calm. *Light in August* comes to us at a much higher temperature than *Sanctuary;* it is an exhaustive analysis of the human disposition (sadistic, masochistic, static) to create and to suffer evil.

The novel begins quietly, peacefully, with scarcely a rumor of the violence to come. Lena Grove appears, on her long voyage from Alabama to seek the father of her child: "a peaceful corridor paved with unflagging and tranquil faith and peopled with kind and nameless faces and voices . . . a long monotonous succession of peaceful and undeviating changes from day to dark and dark to day again, through which she advanced in identical and anonymous and deliberate wagons as though through a succession of creakwheeled and limpeared avatars, like something moving forever and without progress across an urn" (*LA*, 6). As the wagon approaches Jefferson, the driver points from the top of the hill to two fires rising from the landscape: they are the smoke from the saw mill and the fire burning the house of murdered Joanna Burden. Thus the two phases of the novel are joined: Lena, untouched by the violence, lives in and moves through it. The center of violent action is Jefferson, the site of the second column of smoke seen by her from a distance.

The next chapters establish the source of the violence. Joe Christmas enters the tale. He is an astonishing character, the grimmest and most obsessive in Faulkner's work. Alfred Kazin has justly described him as "an abstraction seeking to become a human being . . . the most solitary character in American fiction, the most extreme phase conceivable of American loneliness. . . ."[5] The great tragic force in Joe Christmas comes from the clash of his private world and the world at large. He tries to assert himself from the inner self outward in terms of a recognizable, systematic set of moral standards and sanctions. Since these are not made available or are at best contradictory, he invites and forces violence to his person, in terms of the ambiguities of blood, Negro or White, which he assumes quite voluntarily (there is never any evidence of Negro blood) in his role as a willed martyr, scapegoat, perverted Christ figure.

The Christmas story begins in an orphanage (he is five years old) where he has gone to the dietitian's room to taste her toothpaste; there, hidden behind a screen, he is interrupted by her arrival and her lovemaking with an intern. When she discovers him there, her thin, furious voice hisses out: "You little rat! Spying on me: You little nigger bastard!"

> . . . It never occurred to her that he believed that he was the one who had been taken in sin and was being tortured with punishment deferred and that he was putting himself in her way in order to get it over with, get his whipping and strike the balance and write it off (107).

His confusion is increased when she offers him a silver dollar as a bribe: "He was still with astonishment, shock, outrage . . ." (109).

When she cannot bribe him to keep him from telling what he never understood anyway, he is taken away by a hard, bitter, self-righteous Presbyterian, Simon McEachern. Here at least, despite Christmas's hatred of him, he takes some pleasure in known punishments for recognized misdoing. The balance is at least kept. The dietitian had called him a "nigger bastard"; to this "discovery" McEachern now adds his doctrine of the elect and the damned, thus mixing the Calvinist harshness with the problem of race and blood.[6] But he falls in love with a waitress and prostitute in town, "Bobbie" Allen, and rejects the rigid disciplinarianism of McEachern in favor of her love. The choice is not easy; it is accompanied by an agony of self-growth and by visions of a woman's "filth and abominations."

Joe's love inspires him to murder McEachern; and, when "Bobbie" turns against him with words that are simply a profane and obscene improvement upon the dietitian's, the spell is finally and irrevocably broken. "He stepped from the dark porch, into the moonlight, and with his bloody head and his empty stomach hot, savage, and courageous with whisky, he entered the street which was to run for fifteen years" (195). The two major lessons of his experience are now joined: self-definition is a brutal, harsh, forcibly derived experience, akin to the worst abstractions of Christian law; love is a softness, a weakness, and a deception. Joe Christmas therefore travels the street that "was to run for fifteen years," forcing his experience, demanding his identity, goading and hurting, and doing violence to all soft, weak, contradictory creatures.

Eventually the street runs into Jefferson and to the house of Joanna Burden. No such meeting of violently dedicated and obsessed persons had ever before been contrived, nor is its equal likely to appear. It is the supreme test of the Calvinist conscience, an absolute drama of the breakdown of its invincible convictions. Joe Christmas, whose self-identity has now been violently asserted—forced from within—is now faced with a woman whose being has been forced from without. Each of them is afflicted by a burden, an assumed martyrdom; each of them is firm, violent, and tortured by an inner fear of corruption. Like him, she is obsessed by the burden of the Negro race: he, as imagined victim; she, as imagined heiress of the guilt complex. But the struggle is titanic and vicious: each must force upon the other his conception of what a Negro is. When they make love, he forces her "Negro" will upon her; she whispers "Nigger! Nigger!" in an agony of masochistic triumph. But she must also make him over into the "proper kind of Negro," whose reform is an acquittal of her obligations to the type. When she tries to force him to kneel and pray to her Calvinist God and he refuses, they both know that "there's just one other thing to do" (245).

The deed is death. As he approaches to kill her, her right hand holds "an old style, single action, cap-and-ball revolver almost as long and heavier than a small rifle" (247); and this relic of Civil War times symbolizes the moment when all of this sense of burden and obligation had been crystallized. The gesture is a way of her collaborating in her death, making it (and the lynching of Christmas that is to follow) a unified act of the two of them. He has reached a stage of "immolation," is now specifically marked as the Negro murderer of a white woman; and the weird drama now has its final clues. When, after days and nights of hiding from Negroes, hiding with them, exploding in violent hatred of them, he finally gives himself up in neighboring Mottstown, "It looked like he had set out to get himself caught like a man might set out to get married" (306).

The paths of Joe Christmas and Gail Hightower join. Absorbed in his own static vision of heroism, Hightower has refused on all but one occasion to participate in life. He refuses now to provide Christmas with an alibi. Since he has been a minister, a defrocked man of the pulpit, Hightower's act of refusal may be called another criticism of doctrinal Christianity.[7] At any rate, his fixation in the Southern past makes him insensitive to the quality of human need and experience. When Christmas, fleeing the avenging whites, takes refuge in Hightower's house, he beats Hightower brutally, dropping him to the floor. This is a final expression of Christmas's humanity; like his treatment of Joanna Burden, it testifies to his violent reaction to persons who will deny him this humanity. The death occurs immediately afterward, at the hands of Percy Grimm. At this time Faulkner makes of Christmas a martyr-reminder of a continuing "burden"; the guilt of the South is increased and not assuaged by acts of inhuman violence.

> [The black blood] seemed to rush out of his pale body like a rush of sparks from a rising rocket; upon that black blast the man seemed to rise soaring into their memories forever and ever. They are not to lose it, in whatever peaceful valleys, beside whatever placid and reassuring streams of old age, in the mirroring faces of whatever children they will contemplate old disasters and newer hopes. It will be there, musing, quiet, steadfast, not fading and not particularly threatful, but of itself alone serene, of itself alone triumphant . . . (407).

The death of Joe Christmas culminates a subtle mingling of the legend of the Negro with the psychological drive and compulsion which are its moving force. Joe's assumption of Negrohood is motivated by his experience in seeking and failing clearly to find his identity. But, in assuming it, he must also partake of and force himself into the violence of its effects. He runs into all of the public "myths," stereotypes of what a Negro is: the cliché of mob reaction; the complicated myth of moral responsibility; the arid, sterile fixation of Hightower's withdrawal from humanity; and finally the vengeful "fascist-bred" brutality of Percy Grimm. As Mrs. Vickery has said, "in the process of unfolding of this interaction [of the private and public myths of "Negro"] the chronological sequence has shown the gradual identification of the individual, Joe Christmas, with this public myth . . ." (*Novels*, 74).[8]

The novel ends in a mood of comic simplicity. Lena Grove and Byron Bunch (a latter-day, non-Christian, common man's holy family) travel into Tennessee—"a fur piece"; and their behavior is reported in lusty, comic tones, by the truck driver who had helped them along the way. Yet the novel as a whole has suggested the contrast of Lena and Joe: a pattern of contrasts—peace and fury, stillness and violence—persists throughout. The imagery is maneuvered into a strange kind of strategic attack upon abstract and institutional "goodness." The natural scenes suggest a placidness and an ease of conscience that evoke Lena's indifference to violence. Violence itself occurs in the noisy world of artificial sounds that upset the human balance. Those who turn away from nature suffer violence from their distortions of life or their withdrawal from it.

Alfred Kazin has said that *Light in August* is a novel of original sin, where there is no compensating divine love (*Three Decades*, 263). Lena Grove proves a substitute for it. But her "holiness" is of the earth earthy, comically dainty and wholly mundane. The principal function of the space devoted to Lena Grove is not to show an "alternate way," but to demonstrate the indifference of nature to the colossal errors of men and institutions in their reading and their expropriation of it. Lena Grove proves, if anything, that these social pretensions are not necessary, or at least that it is possible to exist without them.

III

In their special ways, *Sanctuary* and *Light in August* are studies of the projections of evil from the inner self, motivated by a desire to impose the self upon society, as against the will to remain unimpeded and unexploited. The vision of the South as a whole (or of human society itself) as a creation of this selfish and impulsive drive comes in *Absalom, Absalom!* —or is at least part of its meaning. Ilse Dusoir Lind describes the novel as "a grand tragic vision of historic dimension," and then says that its hero falls because of an "innate deficiency of moral insight." Since Sutpen's error is also by extension a social one, his life becomes a "representative anecdote" of tragic human failure.[9]

As legend, representative anecdote, exemplum, or whatever it may be called, the story of Thomas Sutpen, rescued from the views of several narrators, emerges in some such order and chronology as this. In 1817 at age ten, he is living in the mountain country of Virginia, entirely unaware that he is poor or of what it means to be or to want to be rich: "Because where he lived the land belonged to anybody and everybody and so the man who would go to the trouble and work to fence off a piece of it and say 'This is mine' was crazy . . ." (*Absalom,* 221).

But the family moves to the Tidewater lands, and Sutpen has his first glimpse of the privileges of wealth. But even now he does not envy them, or particularly want them, until his father sends him with a message to the big house, and he is stopped at the front door by a Negro servant in full livery, who tells him he must never come to the front door again. The incident suddenly and radically changes him from a boy wanting no privilege to a man wanting all. This is the beginning of the "design," which is at first a desire simply to change the arrangement at the front door: *he* will be the man who owns the house (or one like it) and the Negro servants, who will tell others to go to the back door. Sutpen changes from a state of innocence to one of wild ambition. He needs to have power and to prove to his Negroes that he can dominate them. The "design" takes him at first to Haiti, where he builds a fortune, marries, has a family. But he discovers that his wife has some Negro blood, abandons her, leaves the island, and vanishes from sight for some years. "I found that she was not," he later says to Quentin Compson's grandfather, "and could never be, through no fault of her own, adjunctive or incremental to the design . . ." (240). He has summarily rejected the past in his anxiety to fulfill perfectly a design. This is the real "flaw" in his planning, a flaw he cannot find or understand. He rejects humanity, dismisses his own personal, human commitment.

Sutpen reappears, this time in Jefferson in 1833, at the age of twenty-seven. Once again, he sets about rebuilding, this time he hopes without a flaw. He chooses his wife carefully, Ellen Coldfield, of the most primly respectable and most religious family in Jefferson. He acquires land (one hundred square miles of it northwest of Jefferson); kidnaps a French architect; and, with his aid and that of some thirty Negroes brought with him from Haiti, builds a plantation mansion.

This time the design seems near completion; but, though Sutpen has set aside the past, it returns to haunt him. His son of the first marriage, Charles Bon, arrives; falls in love with Judith, of the second marriage; and the families are dangerously near being unified in an incestuous relationship. The Civil War intervenes, and Charles Bon and Henry Sutpen (the two sons of two different marriages) go to fight with or near their father. When the war is over, Charles and Henry ride to the gate of Sutpen's Hundred, where Henry kills Charles because of the threat of incest and miscegenation the marriage holds.

Once again Sutpen is foiled, his children killed or in hiding, his estate reduced to nothing, he himself reduced to running a crossroads store. He makes two more attempts to restore the family. First, he proposes to Rosa Coldfield that they live together and, if she gives him a male heir, promises he will marry her. When she indignantly rejects him, he then tries to gain a son through Milly Jones, daughter of his old retainer. Their child is a daughter, and Sutpen then goads Wash Jones to kill him. He has failed again and again, because he has arbitrarily dismissed human values. The sons want something other than abstract power; and, in looking beyond it, they upset his drive for power. Since he has left humanity out of his plans, it is responsible for the "flaws" in his design.[10]

This is the narrative of Sutpen, but it is not the novel. *Absalom* is not the story, but the meaning it has for those who tell it. The novel is intricately constructed from the knowledge of these narrators, each of whom has a particular individual perspective compounded of special knowledges and a special ignorance. In the beginning Rosa Coldfield tells her version to Quentin Compson just before his departure for Harvard. For her Sutpen is "the evil's source and head which had outlasted all its victims . . ." (18). She had grown up in "a grim mausoleum of Puritan righteousness and outraged female vindictiveness . . ." (60). She has herself been wearing black for forty-three years and has shut herself up in the "dim coffin-smelling gloom" of an unventilated and darkened room; she exudes "the rank smell of female old flesh long embattled in virginity" (8).

The story in her perspective is charged with her special hatreds and prejudices. Sutpen was *"this demon"* who had "abrupted" from nowhere into Jefferson, "torn violently a plantation," and begot a son and daughter upon her sister Ellen (9). She wants to prove that God has brought defeat to the South because He wished to purge it of the "demon." Nothing in the account is told quietly, or graciously, or with charity. Everything was done by him for entirely vicious reasons. In her haste to condemn him, she ignores or shows her ignorance of facts: Sutpen's forbidding the marriage of Charles Bon and Judith, for example, was "without rhyme or reason or shadow of excuse . . ." (18). Because of Sutpen's slighting of Bon, she is inordinately fond of him though she has never known or even seen him: "I heard a name, I saw a photograph, I helped to make a grave and that was all . . ." (146).

The second version of the tale—Quentin's father and his grandfather share it—provides external details. Sutpen doesn't "explode into Jefferson from nowhere"; he arrives on a Sunday morning in 1833 and pays court to Ellen Coldfield. There are curious and strange things in the man's behavior and his past is never clearly understood, but there is no especial predisposition either for or against him. In other words, Quentin's father is the outside observer, curious, indulgent, but not well informed because he is scarcely able to penetrate beneath the surface. He is hopelessly at a loss to explain many things, because he is not capable of seeing or appreciating the agony of any Sutpen relationship. He invokes a type of tragic Muse to help him, and sees the Sutpen story as a classical tragedy working inevitably through two generations of passionate failure. But he cannot otherwise explain Sutpen's forbidding the marriage or discover why Henry should have killed Bon. "It's just incredible. It just doesn't explain . . ." (100), he says when he reaches an impasse. So the tragedy of Sutpen is a punishment for *hubris,* in the manner of the Greek tragic hero who is struck down for his arrogance.

Ultimately the story of Sutpen becomes Quentin's own responsibility. With his roommate at Harvard, Shreve McCannon, he tries in the "iron New England dark" to reconstruct it totally from the accounts he has had of it. Since he is a son, the story becomes that of the Sutpen children, responding to the errors and arbitrary decisions of their father. In his zeal to recast the tale, he becomes involved in it; he *becomes* Henry Sutpen on the Civil War battlefront: Quentin and Shreve are assimilated by Charles and Henry: "they were both in North Carolina and the time was 46 years ago . . . both of them were Henry Sutpen and both of them were Bon, compounded each of both and yet either neither . . ." (351). The reasons for Henry's murder of Bon, quite lost to the other narrators, are here a crucial matter: was it the incest or miscegenation? Quentin concludes that it was not the incest (which he could have tolerated, as he can understand his own involvement with Caddy), but the fear of miscegenation. This seems to him to have been borne out in the pitiful decline of Sutpen generations: Jim Bond, the grandson of Charles Bon and his New Orleans mistress, is an idiot Negro; and, with that knowledge, the decline of the Sutpens seems not unlike the decline of the Compsons with Benjy, "child of mine old age."

In the novel's concluding passage, Shreve turns to Quentin and asks, "Why do you hate the South?" Quentin protests; "I dont hate it," he says,

quickly, at once, immediately; "I dont hate it," he said. *I dont hate it* he thought, panting in the cold air, the iron New England dark; *I dont. I dont! I dont hate it! I dont hate it!*"

The ambiguities of his declaration are a perfect summing up of the novel's meaning. In each of the Sutpen versions, this hard, passionate demand upon the emotions is present. The story of Sutpen is a model version of the rise of families; and each narrator gives his own sense of the alarm, hatred, pride, and prejudice with which it is viewed or with which he participates in it. Quentin is here considering his heritage as of "a barracks filled with stubborn back-looking ghosts still recovering, even forty-three years afterward, from the fever which had cured the disease. . . ," or "an empty hall echoing with sonorous defeated names . . ." (12). He both loves and hates it. He does not know if the dedication to his past is worth either his love or his hatred, so he must cry out in the "iron New England dark" his despair of ever coming to terms with it.

Absalom is a full review of the South as a representative kind of experience. The evil emerges, as it did not in *Sanctuary*, from an inspired determination to duplicate a poorly understood but a passionately desired good. There are slips and twists and turns in the process—the "flaws in the design"— to which Quentin and the others must turn their attention. It is impossible either to reject or to accept it totally. *Absalom* was the only novel in which Faulkner reviewed the total cultural pattern of the South and then offered a number of insights into its effects upon those who, involved in it yet misunderstanding or hating a part or much of it, must somehow come to terms with it. As such, the novel is an admirable means of viewing his thematic preoccupations and concerns, which are examined elsewhere in more specific detail and in their several layers and levels of application.

CHAPTER 5

The Negro and the Folk

I

THREE BOOKS deserve brief notices before we move on to the final period of Faulkner's work: *Pylon* (1935), which returns to aviation, one of Faulkner's earliest interests, and is in several respects an attempt to write a "modern novel"; *The Unvanquished* (1938), a series of stories that are really very close to being a novel, which concern the growth of Bayard Sartoris from Civil War days to the crucial period of the Reconstruction; and *The Wild Palms* (1939), a brilliant experiment in the interweaving of two apparently separate stories.

Pylon, in the modern idiom (there are many suggestions of Faulkner's literary *milieu*), concerns the career of a group of stunt and racing pilots; the occasion is the dedication of New Valois, the New Orleans airport. Its principal characters are Roger Shumann, the pilot of an old "crate," which he causes to perform prodigies of speed; Laverne, his woman and eventually his wife, whom he has picked up on one of his flying circus junkets; and Jack, a parachute jumper who shares Laverne's bed with Shumann. In the course of events, Shumann crashes the plane, which he does not own but flies on commission; manages to get another through the efforts of a reporter; and dies when that crashes into Lake Pontchartrain.

Faulkner seems to want to present in *Pylon* the curiously intense, concentrated, weirdly unconventional lives of persons dedicated to an age of speed *per se*. The life is unconventional in every respect, the people are always on edge, they live quick and intense lives, they pay no real respect to the world that surrounds them and offers them prizes for their mechanical acrobatics.

Faulkner had said in a review of *Test Pilot,* a book by one of the stunt fliers of these days, that he was trying to catch the beginnings of a folklore of "the high speed of today," or at least that he wanted to translate the speed itself into the rhythms and pace of a novel.[1] The reporter, who serves often the role of point of view, gives *Pylon* its eccentric character: in love with Laverne, or infatuated, he takes the strange group under his "protection," tries to live a life similar to theirs, and ends merely by helping to destroy its leader. Far from being an Eliot character (there are suggestions of both "Prufrock" and *The Waste Land* in the novel), he is another of the aberrant, partly confused and partly grotesque characters in Faulkner's novels who grope toward the meaning of a life they do not understand.

The wild unceremoniousness of Shumann's group—its frenzy of late nights, drink, emergencies, and sexual confusion—seems to be Faulkner's analogue of the speed and excitement of flying itself. The analogy takes substance from the exposure of these people to public gaze. They are on view in performances and circuses which are a mixture of spectator lust and carnival. Laverne is on view as she is on call. Faulkner's hostility to modernism is further demonstrated; for, as in *Sanctuary* and in suggestions in other novels, he shows a strong opposition to speed, spectatorial lust and pleasure, and mechanical limitations of the real.

Shumann, however, seems a fully realized scapegoat of these modern tendencies. Donald Torchiana and John R. Marvin suggest Shumann as a Christ figure. His death, Torchiana says, is an act of redemption and "grace": "Shumann's act partially redeems the guilt of all men. One feels that the ferro-concrete world of city and airport has trembled and is momentarily calmed and emptied of its terror."[2] Whether these suggestions of *Waste Land* and New Testament are useful or not, the figure of Shumann is an important reminder that Faulkner is, in *Pylon* as elsewhere, intent upon finding the "saving grace" in a world that without it collapses into meaningless chaos. Shumann is perhaps even more convincing in the role than Gavin Stevens: he says little, acts with urgency but unselfishly, and dies for a conviction he spends little time in verbalizing. But the attempt to transfer his values into a non-Yoknapatawpha world is not wholly successful. The pace is frenetic, and there is no cultural frame in which to consider men's actions. The pylon of course is a grotesque parody of symbolism, around which both planes and men revolve. Faulkner's uneasy hatred of the "pure present" causes him to create in *Pylon* an extremely interesting but a somehow inadequate and incomplete novel.

The Unvanquished is once again back in the myth and circumstance of his County. Not a novel, it nevertheless holds a line of consistent relevance to a group of representative people; it is more, therefore, than a mere "collection" of short stories. The early stories are almost "slick" scenes in the lives of Bayard Sartoris and his Negro friend Ringo, who talk and conspire near the end of the Civil War. They also concern the redoubtable "Granny Millard."

The book moves into the post-Civil War Reconstruction scene and the Sartoris involvement in it; there are many echoes and anticipations of other novels: *Sartoris, Light in August, The Hamlet.* The final story, "Odor of Verbena," brings to a crisis whatever issue the book has suggested. However romantic the conclusion may be, it genuinely puts the moral problem of killing to the test. The death of Bayard's father is not viewed by his son as a mere romantic culmination of heroism. It is regarded and judged skeptically; and the book, which has at times risked the most superficial of romantic meanings, closes on a note of somber meditation about the motives men have for killing each other. From the perspective of "The Odor of Verbena," we realize (almost for the first time) that the earlier stories are viewed as in the past—and also morally judged.

The crisis in the Sartoris life is, therefore, a crisis in the "legend" of the South. How much of the heroics are necessary? Are they meaningful, or an unsettling of emotional dust? The young boy (who in *Sartoris* is an old man of prestige and substance) grows up living in and with a set of attitudes toward action and heroism. In his experience as participant but especially as observer, he has to reshape the legend in his own way in order to live with it. He does what the boys and the old woman of *Intruder* do: he tries to reduce a stance of bluster and romantic impulse and violence to a common human denominator. His boyhood experiences strike him at first as romantically exciting; but somehow the passage of time gives them a new character. The behavior of family and friends is finally judged for what it is: often shrewd, sometimes ingenious and impulsive, but not always right or just.

The young Bayard is left at the end of *The Unvanquished* as the heir to the family's traditional status; but he is also left with a modified view of what constitutes tradition. As a man moving into the modern world, he will not have an easy life, but he will not be recklessly or nonsensically "heroic" in defending the Sartoris position. *The Unvanquished* thus is a link of Sartoris past with Sartoris future; at the same time, it is a judgment upon the one and a clear view ahead of the other. If Faulkner's work were viewed in terms of the sequence of his examinations of the past and present of the County, *The Unvanquished* would stand significantly at or near the head of it.[3]

The true distinction of *The Wild Palms* comes from its having alternated two apparently disparate stories: that of the "tall convict," who is caught in the confusion of a Mississippi flood; and that of Harry Wilbourne, an intern, and Charlotte Rittenmeyer, two lovers "against the world." The two stories seem unrelated, and most critics have refused to consider them as having any significant relationship. Malcolm Cowley went so far as to ignore one of them altogether; subsequent reprintings have often printed them separately; and a paperback edition published them as consistent but separate stories.[4] Faulkner has, however, been quite explicit about their inter-relationship; in his discussions at the University of Virginia, 1957–58, he said:

> The story I was trying to tell was the story of Charlotte and Harry Wilbourne. I decided that it needed a contrapuntal quality like music. And so I wrote the other story simply to underline the story of Charlotte and Harry. I wrote the two stories by alternate chapters. I'd write the chapter of one and then I would write the chapter of the other just as the musician puts in—puts counterpoint behind the theme that he is working with (*Faulkner in the University,* 171).

Perhaps the major reason for taking the form seriously is that both stories play upon a central theme of human freedom: not upon freedom itself, but upon the intricate psychological problems involved in wanting it, experiencing it, or repudiating the desire of it. The tall convict, shocked into realizing the serious responsibilities involved in decisions freely made, simply rejects every opportunity the rampaging waters of "Old Man" Mississippi provide him; Wilbourne and Charlotte "take" their freedom but have to pay eventually for the privilege of it—she in death and he in imprisonment.

Both Wilbourne and the tall convict end in the prison farm at Parchman. Mrs. Vickery very shrewdly observes that "both Parchman prison in which the tall convict is serving his sentence and the hospital where Harry Wilbourne is an interne are microcosmic images of society which must of necessity impose limitations on personal freedom for the sake of order" (*Novels,* 156-57). The two settings and situations are joined in the fact that they first set limits upon human freedom, then (because of choice or accident) offer opportunities to violate order and push freedom a far way, and finally suggest that man must return to a condition of order. It is chosen freely by the tall convict but forced upon Wilbourne.

Faulkner's ingenious pattern is brilliantly supported by the contrasting but somehow convincingly complementary scenes of hospital and flood. The hospital is an ever-present reminder of the consequences of excess; the flood is, broadly and violently, excess pure and simple. Nature will go where it will, as the "Old Man" testifies; man must protect himself from its excesses as best he can. Charlotte's death, because of a clumsily unsuccessful abortion, is a further testimony of the ironic limits it puts upon human freedom. And Parchman prison, which forces order upon those who have recklessly chosen freedom, becomes the end of the road for both central figures of the novel. *The Wild Palms* has not received adequate attention, perhaps because it impressed the critics when published as an eccentric and—at least on the surface—scarcely useful experiment.

II

The reason for suggesting that a third, and as it turns out, a final period of Faulkner's work began in 1940 is the publication in that year of *The Hamlet*, the first of a trilogy describing the career of the Snopes "tribe." Beyond this fact, we find that he has in the 1940's concerned himself with related problems, which may be joined with the phrase "the Negro and the Folk." The "folk" are in this case the tenant farmers, their wry and knowing spokesmen, and their exploiters. Neither the folk nor the Negro is a new phenomenon in Faulkner's fiction, but for a few years he concentrates upon them as if he had decided they needed full treatment. Both Negro and folk are victims of exploitation from without and of weaknesses and indecision from within.

Faulkner describes the tenant farmers in one of his characteristically brilliant, inclusive, and incisive passages at the very opening of *The Hamlet*:

> . . . [They] came from the northeast, through the Tennessee mountains by stages marked by the bearing and raising of a generation of children. They came from the Atlantic seaboard and before that, from England and the Scottish and Welsh Marches, as some of the names would indicate—Turpin and Haley and Whittington, McCallum and Murray and Leonard and Littlejohn . . . They brought no slaves and no Phyfe and Chippendale highboys; indeed, what they did bring most of them could (and did) carry in their hands. They took up land

and built one- and two-room cabins and never painted them,
and married one another and produced children and added
other rooms one by one to the original cabins and did not
paint them either, but that was all. . . . Federal officers went
into the country and vanished. . . . They supported their own
churches and schools, they married and committed infrequent
adulteries and more frequent homicides among themselves and
were their own courts, judges and executioners. They were
Protestants and Democrats and prolific; there was not one
Negro landowner in the entire section. Strange Negroes would
absolutely refuse to pass through it after dark.[5]

These are the white citizens of Frenchman's Bend, a hamlet
some twenty miles southeast of Jefferson. They had been ruled
with benevolent, political tyranny by the Varner family, who
exploited them, knew their weaknesses and took advantage
of them, but, in spite of everything, lived in comparative
amity and profitable peace with them. The Varners' victims
scarcely thought of themselves as such. They were hard-
working; spoke their own minds, or thought they did; and en-
joyed the easy, slow comradeship of the long, tall tale, or the
quiet tobacco-chewing session on the "gallery" of the store,
or the "excitement" of an annual circus-sale of wild ponies
from Texas. They were not looking for trouble, but they were
also wildly impulsive and irrational: their desires for gain and
for excitement, their frustrations, and their quickness to anger
suggested a sub-rational fury and intensity which, combined
with a naïve trustfulness, made them the perfect victims of less
emotional and shrewder minds.

The Hamlet is not only a study of them in depth; it is also,
and pre-eminently, an analysis of the Snopes family—and of
Snopesism as a human and social type. There are many de-
grees of Snopesism in The Hamlet, ranging from "pure" Snopes
(Flem) to adulterated Snopes (Mink) to non-Snopes (Eck).
The pure Snopes is shrewd and cunning and deceptive and
amoral; he is also a consistent and "dedicated" and "logical"
man (in the sense in which Faulkner describes Jason Compson
as "logical"). He possesses integrity, if that word be narrowly
defined.

Mrs. Vickery has given us what is perhaps the most pene-
trating characterization of Flem, the major representative of
the Snopes absolute:

> . . . he is a comic version of Thomas Sutpen forcing his way
> into an ordered and hierarchical society and confronting it
> with his own mirror images. Both, to some extent, share the
> same innocence which consists of acting in terms of a design,
> the one social and the other economic, from which all vital
> instincts and feelings have been eliminated. Thus through
> Flem's exclusive preoccupation with business, the nature and
> limitations of the economic man and of the ethics of business
> are demonstrated. For Flem . . . does have ethics, but they are
> ethics concerned with a ledger rather than with people . . .
> (*Novels*, 169-70).

That Flem Snopes has these clearly defined lines of personality does not, of course, diminish the fact of Faulkner's
criticizing his kind, presenting the human farce of its denial
of humanity, and ultimately passing judgment upon the total
negation of human "verities" it stands for.[6] This criticism partly enables Faulkner to use his remarkable sense of comedy
and farce. At the same time they are feared, Snopeses are ridiculed even by the name given them. As Harry Campbell and
Reuel Foster have pointed out, the sound of *Snopes* com-
municates a quality ugly and snarling and fearsome (sneak,
snoop, snake, sneer, etc.); for it is almost impossible to as-
sociate the "sn" sound at the beginning of a word with anything pleasant. Snopes "is a caricature of all 'sn-ishness' in
human nature."[7]

Not only the surname, but the variety of given names suggest generic qualities. Flem (phlegm), as a "mucous discharge
from the mouth" expresses or induces contempt and disgust.
Other Snopes names, along with personal descriptions, run the
gamut of predatory animals, which stands in vivid contrast
to the "gift of nature" as Ratliff sees it. Campbell and Foster
note that Flem is seen as froglike; I.O., as a weasel; Lancelot
(Lump), ratlike; St. Elmo, goatlike. Mink Snopes has a name
that defines itself (105).

One passage provides a comical summary of Snopes predatoriness: St. Elmo is caught stealing candy from the store's supply; Jody Varner describes him as "worse than a goat."

". . . First thing I know, he'll graze on back and work through that lace leather and them hame-strings and lap-links and ring-bolts and eat me and you and him all three clean out the back door. And then be damned if I wouldn't be afraid to turn my back for fear he would cross the road and start in on the gin and the blacksmith shop . . ." (*The Hamlet,* 323-24).

To protect the folk from this fearsome, omnivorous tribe, Faulkner sets up the figure of V. K. Ratliff, an itinerant sewing-machine salesman, who is the representative of articulate humanity, a rational "good" man, and one of imaginative sympathy. He shrewdly observes and appraises the "invasion" of Frenchman's Bend, and even at times to combat it on its own terms. But he is able to go only so far; his is not the pure good that can resolutely struggle against pure evil. He has his relapses into the irrational and becomes himself a victim of Snopes chicanery.

If Ratliff stands above the irrational impulse of the folk, Henry Armstid stands supremely for its deepest and most powerful drives; and the two of them, digging and searching for treasure Flem Snopes has trapped them into thinking exists on the Old Frenchman's place, have a common bond of impulse and gullibility in the novel's farcical conclusion.

Nevertheless, as Faulkner's specimen of the "humanist"—the man aware of human frailties, yet usually able to transcend them—Ratliff does give the world of Snopes a gauge and a pair of scales. He is in the hamlet from time to time as his business requires, filling in details for himself, and spinning the Snopes fact into a comically imaginative succession of yarns, fables, and sermons. Ratliff is the journeyman humanist; his wisdom is folk-wisdom; and his life is that of a man who sells to the folk but does not "sell them out." He goes only so far; his sense of outrage does not betray him into the role of purist hero or secular saint. Near the end of *The Hamlet* he eloquently explains why he will not (and cannot) go the whole way:

> ". . . I wasn't protecting a Snopes from Snopeses; I wasn't even protecting a people from a Snopes. I was protecting something that wasn't even a people, that wasn't nothing but something that dont want nothing but to walk and feel the sun and wouldn't know how to hurt no man even if it would and wouldn't want to even if it could . . . I never made them Snopeses and I never made the folks that cant wait to bare their backsides to them. I could do more, but I wont. I wont. I tell you!" (326).

Snopeses have appeared in the County before; as small-time shysters or politicians, they are a part of the landscape of *Sartoris* and *Sanctuary;* they appear as bushwackers behind the lines of Civil War battles, favoring no one and exploiting any who have the will to be "sold" in *The Unvanquished.* As *The Hamlet* begins, the older Snopes generation, more mildly and more generously described, has been "soured" by losing in a trade. The Varners, closer to the older Snopeses than they at first seem, are casually acquisitive and venially wicked; but they are no match for the tribe of which Flem is titular head but scarcely the leader. In the beginning, it is the threat of barn-burning that gives the alien tribe a foothold. It is then a matter of time before they will take over the store, the cotton gin, the schoolhouse, and then move on to Jefferson and the bank and the mansion.

Flem begins as a clerk in the Varner store: ". . . a thick squat soft man of no establishable age between twenty and thirty, with a broad still face containing a tight seam of mouth stained slightly at the corners with tobacco, and eyes the color of stagnant water, and projecting from among other features in startling and sudden paradox, a tiny predatory nose like the beak of a small hawk" (52). In a few months of impeccably accurate and efficient clerking, he has taken over the store and moves over to the gin. He appropriates the Varner business; he puts a Snopes, the garrulous I.O., into the schoolhouse; he takes over the land when he "arranges" to marry

Will Varner's daughter and is deeded the Frenchman's place; and he conquers the law by staying scrupulously within it and cautiously beyond the reach of its protocol. When he moves to Jefferson in *The Town*, he sets his ambition higher, but not too much higher, and, by maneuverings and deals, acquires respectability or its décor in the De Spain mansion. At one point in Flem's progress, Jody Varner asks Ratliff, in a shaking voice:

> "I want to make one pure and simple demand of you and I want a pure Yes and No for a answer: How many more is there? How much longer is this going on? Just what is it going to cost to protect one goddamn barn of hay?" (*The Hamlet*, 68).

Flem goes very far indeed, moving in a straight line toward his objective, never missing a chance to capitalize on his strength and the weaknesses of others. Faulkner, however, has more than one purpose to fulfill; for he wishes to show not only the unilateral triumph of Flem Snopes but the impact of it upon the humanity of Frenchman's Bend and upon the land.⁸ Book two of *The Hamlet* is a comically exaggerated "myth" of the earth and of Eula Varner, its goddess. Eula is rich and full-bodied and easy and instinctively "natural": "some symbology out of the old Dionysic times . . ." (95); "emanating that outrageous quality of being, existing, actually on the outside of the garments she wore and not only being unable to help it but not even caring" (102); "a moist blast of spring's liquorish corruption, a pagan triumphal prostration before the supreme primal uterus" (114). Her first "conquest" is of the schoolmaster Labove, one of Faulkner's great comic creations. Labove has always had a blind and absolute trust in the power of words as the sure and only path to success.⁹ Centuries ago he would have been a monk; now he prepares for the career of lawyer and politician. But the "liquorish corruption" gets in the way of the words, and he is destroyed and ridiculed. Eula, first tempting him by her very presence in the school, then turns him aside in childish contempt.

Eula draws men to her and then repels them—all but one. She is waiting for her "consort," who finally appears in the person of Hoake McCarron. Until his arrival, she is "nucleus of that loud frustrated group" of would-be suitors, "casting over them all that spell of incipient accouchement while refusing herself to be pawed at . . ." (129). But McCarron succeeds where they fail and then disappears. And when the Varners discover that she is "in trouble," they can do nothing but protect the family name; a deal is made to give Eula in marriage to Flem Snopes—with some of the Varner property. This marriage is a parody of the rite. Flem and Eula appear for their "honeymoon" in Texas, the straw suitcase on his knees, "like the coffin of a baby's funeral" (146).

The story of Eula now becomes a folk tale of a land laid waste and given over to impotence. After Eula has gone, Ratliff observes the land given in convenient marriage to its impotent ruler:

> . . . the old, now-glandless earth-creeping, the very buds and blossoms, the garlands of whose yellowed triumphs had long fallen into the profitless dust, enbalmed now and no more dead to the living world if they were sealed in buried vaults . . . (149).

He felt outrage at the waste, "at a situation intrinsically and inherently wrong by any comedy, like building a log dead-fall and baiting it with a freshened heifer to catch a rat . . ." (161-62).

The conquest of Eula is followed by one of the most elaborate parodies in literature of the romantic view of nature's bounty and beauty. This section of the novel is alternately exaggeratedly comic and profound. Flem is gone temporarily; but another Snopes, the idiot Ike, takes over. Ike's idyllic love of the Houston cow, his knight-errantry on behalf of "*la belle vache sans merci*," strikes one at times as impossibly elaborate, at others as unrelievedly sad. Here Eula's female power is all but sadistically reduced to its bovine level, "the flowing immemorial female" (168). But the land itself is victim, "a region of scrubby second-growth pine and oak among which dogwood bloomed until it too was cut to make cotton spindles, and old fields . . . gutted and gullied by forty years of rain and frost and heat into plateaus choked with rank sedge . . ." (174). Upon this deprived landscape Ike and the cow disport themselves. Ike nobly pursues the shy, reluctant female; and the courtship is embellished by a rhetoric that is richly and ironically romantic. Flem's absence from the scene, but above all Eula's capitulation to the Varner family expedient, marks the event and its drama as ultimately pathetic rather than ridiculous.[10]

"The Long Summer" (Book Three) concludes with still another event that is informed more by harsh pathos than by comedy. Again it features a Snopes, but a variant so great as to argue isolation from Snopesism altogether. Mink Snopes possesses, and is a victim of, a power of passion. He is moved by hatred, or in another sense by a fury of resentment pushed as far as it will go. He has been abused and taken advantage of by his neighbor Houston (himself a Faulkner character surcharged with a wondrous, twisted passion), until he kills him, and tries to conceal the body in a nearby swamp. The account of "burial and recapture" is in its enumeration of gruesome detail like some passages in the later *Knight's Gambit*. But its purpose, so far as *The Hamlet* is concerned, is to prove that one Snopes, one *Flem* Snopes, will not protect another. This section concludes in jail with Mink Snopes madly shaking the bars, shouting for Flem to rescue him, and cursing him because he knows it is not to be.

> "I would have been all right," he said, harsh, whispering. Then his voice failed altogether again and he held to the bar with one hand, holding his throat with the other, while the Negroes watched him, huddled, their eyeballs white and still in the failing light . . . (263).

In *The Mansion*, the last novel of the trilogy, Mink's story is reviewed and becomes the crucial event of the Snopes record. Mink is now in the Parchman prison, sent there, he thinks at least, because Flem had not once troubled to help him. Faulkner said to his students at Virginia in 1957–58, before *The Mansion* had appeared though its publication had been rumored, that the Snopeses "will destroy themselves ..."(*Faulkner in the University,* 282). This they do; *The Mansion* describes with admirable fitness what one type of Snopes can do to another. Faulkner remains scrupulously objective, allowing Ratliff, then others, and then the landscape itself to contain the judgment of Flem's career. In *The Town,* many others had had a hand in recounting the increase of Snopeses and the rise of the redoubtable Flem toward his "pinnacle" of respectability. In *The Mansion,* the same citizens of Jefferson, joined now by Eula's daughter (Eula has died), reflect, observe, wonder, arrange, and finally act— or permit action or do not prevent it—to the end that Mink is able to avenge himself for Flem's neglect.

The murder scene is a masterpiece of appropriate and skillful art. In the quality of it—its "serenity" and its stillness—the full length and depth of Snopes treachery and limitation are made precisely meaningful. After years of imprisonment (some of them added by Flem's actions) and after days of an erratic and painful journey south, Mink arrives in Jefferson. Everything seems to conspire against the success of his mission, but it does succeed. Mink finally finds himself in the mansion with the old and unreliable pistol in his right hand and with Flem staring silently, passively at both.

> Now his cousin, his feet now flat on the floor and the chair almost swiveled to face him, appeared to sit immobile and even detached too, watching too Mink's grimed shaking child-sized hands like the hands of a pet coon as one of them lifted the hammer enough for the other to roll the cylinder back one notch so that the shell would come again under the hammer. . .

> It made a tremendous sound though in the same instant Mink no longer heard it. His cousin's body was now making a curious half-stifled surge which in another moment was going to carry the whole chair over. . .[11]

Flem is destroyed by another Snopes, but not before he has fully earned his death. The saga of Snopes triumph must necessarily end this way, as Faulkner has justly said. But in *The Hamlet* Flem is very much alive, and nowhere is his skill in gauging and using circumstance so expertly treated than in the final section, "The Peasants." The passages which delineate the sale of the spotted horses Flem has brought back with him from Texas are the most frequently reprinted of all of Faulkner's work. They represent Flem at his measly best, the "folk" at their most violent and most eager, and Ratliff comically at the end of his strategy. The section begins with circus imagery: the horses appear in the distance like "obviously alive objects which in the levelling sun resembled vari-sized and -colored tatters torn at random from large billboards—circus posters, say . . ." (*The Hamlet*, 275). The scene's most fitting epithets are "gaudy" and "violent," and the two adjectives properly describe not only it but the farmers who are being readied for the sale. The violence is brilliantly rendered by the horses' surging and swinging, by their impulsive and erratic moves forward and back, and by "a kaleidoscopic maelstrom of long teeth and wild eyes and slashing feet" (279).

The people are attracted inevitably to the scene, for Ratliff's efforts to dissuade them are futile. There is something stubborn, convinced, and passive about them, "like children who have been chidden" (282). As Ratliff speaks to them, they simply look away from time toward the "splotchy, sporadic surge and flow of the horses . . ." (283), and think of excuses for what they and Ratliff know no one can prevent their doing. When the day of the sale arrives, they are all gathered there early; and the Texan whom Flem has hired as a blind knows he will have their interest and their money eventually. Only Mrs. Littlejohn, the perfect, sane measuring rod of the proceedings, goes about her regular tasks with an occasional muttered comment about "those men."

In a "brisk loud unemphatic mixture of cursing and cajolery" (287), the Texan has both ponies and men within his reach and can maneuver human greeds against each other. He is a center of strength surrounded by a colorful, swirling mass of ponies and men: ". . . a kaleidoscope of inextricable and incredible violence on the periphery of which the metal clasps of the Texan's suspenders sun-glinted in ceaseless orbit . . ." (293). To represent the compulsive willingness of the men to buy, Faulkner has provided an extreme example in Henry Armstid; the man who had played bit parts in *As I Lay Dying* and *Light in August* becomes now a monster of determined greed. When his wife protests mildly because he has the family's last and only five dollars, "The man turned upon her with that curious air of leashed, of dreamlike fury" (295).

By five o'clock the sale is finished and the Texan has gone. Now the animals and the men "for an instant of static horror . . . faced one another, then the men whirled and ran before a gaudy vomit of long wild faces . . ." (306). The result is a chase in the moonlight for fleeing ponies, two accidents, some brief but wild encounters, and two lawsuits against Flem Snopes, which are dismissed for lack of definite evidence.

Before this chase Faulkner's sense of comedy has a wide, free range. The fleeing ponies head in every direction. One of them plunges into the Littlejohn yard and moves quickly into the house itself:

A lamp sat on a table just inside the door. In its mellow light they saw the horse fill the long hallway like a pinwheel, gaudy, furious and thunderous. A little further down the hallway there was a varnished yellow melodeon. The horse crashed into it; it produced a single note, almost a chord, in bass, resonant and grave, of deep and sober astonishment; the horse with its monstrous and antic shadow whirled again and vanished through another door. It was a bedroom; Ratliff, in his underclothes and one sock and with the other sock in his hand and his back to the door, was leaning out the open window facing the lane, the lot. He looked back over his shoulder. For an instant he and the horse glared at one another. Then he sprang through the window as the horse backed out of the room and into the hall again . . . (307-308).

III

Faulkner's concern with the Negro is pervasive in his novels, but in the 1940's he attended especially to the deep-rooted uneasiness and the erratic violence of assertion involved in Negro-White relationships. These are never entirely isolated, for they are much involved with the question of the land itself, not only symbolically but as a problem of moral economics.

Go Down, Moses is an example of this far-reaching exploration. Its major dramatic concern is the relationship of Isaac McCaslin, the white hunter and recluse, and Lucas Beauchamp, mulatto son of McCaslin's grandfather. Combined with the obvious opportunities such a situation presents are the moral questions of miscegenation, the matter of racial origins, the symbolic meaning of wilderness, and the ritual implications of the hunt. While Lucas is quite fully developed in *Go Down, Moses*, his moment of greatest drama is reserved for *Intruder in the Dust*. Meanwhile, the central obligation of the earlier book is Ike's, and the most important treatment of it is the famous story "The Bear."

In its larger implications, the killing of the bear is the crucial event. It is ambiguous in meaning, but it is surely not intended to advise a return to a primitive culture or to condemn superficially the destruction of the wilderness. Rather, Faulkner seems to say that the killing of the bear is a necessary event, that we cannot rewrite history or reverse the direction of man, but that we must assert "humanity" in all its complex of doubt, aberrant weakness, and remorse. In the killing, the bear and the slayers play the complex role of the figures on Keats's Grecian urn: in reality and life, they seem at times remote from Keats's meaning, but beauty and truth and goodness emerge from the highest and most crucial moment of their engagement with humanity.

The story opens with Ike McCaslin sixteen years old and then maneuvers back and forth in his years to develop and emphasize his growth to maturity. The most important lesson of his experience has to do with the semi-religious identity of the wilderness with the bear. Faulkner is suggesting that their ages are roughly similar and that the hacking away of the wilderness corresponds to the bear's decline. But both bear and wilderness are "eternal," if one can fix upon a moment in which they give most richly of their essential quality. This moment is the death of the bear, but it is preceded by a number of events in the young life of Ike, who has to learn slowly the craft and the ceremony of hunting and woodsmanship.

The spectacle of the "little puny humans" gnawing away at the woods—"men myriad and nameless even to one another in the land where the bear had earned a name"[12]—corresponds to the discoveries Ike later makes of the venality and pettiness of men as he prepares to give up his heritage. Ike is present at the killing of Big Ben; he sees it as a moment not only of great crisis but also of high and permanent art. The old hunter Boon Hogganbeck, the dog Lion, and the bear take part in a *tableau*:

> It fell just once. For an instant they almost resembled a piece of statuary: the clinging dog, the bear, the man astride its back, working and probing the buried blade. Then they went down, pulled over backward by Boon's weight, Boon underneath. . . . It didn't collapse, crumple. It fell all of a piece, as a tree falls, so that all three of them, man dog and bear, seemed to bounce once (*Moses*, 241).

When Ike discovers from the records in the store the true story of his grandfather's sins of incest and miscegenation, he feels that he must somehow make restitution, for the meaning of his initiation in the hunting would otherwise be made to seem futile.[13] The land is actually not his to repudiate, he says; it is not any man's for it is merely given him by God in trust. This is a version of the Eden image, and Ike otherwise assumes an attitude of biblical wisdom re-enacted in the lives of men.

In the elaborate rhetoric of Part Four, Faulkner offers a variety of "meanings," the most important of which are the following: (1) The land is not man's to do with what he pleases but a kind of "responsible Eden," a divinely ordained "second chance" for man. (2) The burden of the races is inseparable from that responsibility; all three races—Indians, Negroes, and whites—must live together on the land (the friendship of Sam Fathers, who is both Indian and Negro, with Ike in his youth is especially important) and any violation of that responsibility (like that of which Ike's grandfather is guilty) brings a curse upon the responsible one. (3) The hunt is a formal manner of expressing the relationship of man and nature. (4) The lives of men have suggestions of eternal beauty and meaning in moments of highest emotion and most vital importance.

Such a moment is apprehended by Ike McCaslin and his cousin, when they discuss Keats's Ode. *"He was talking* about truth," his cousin says of Keats. *". . . It covers all things which touch the heart—honor and pride and pity and justice and courage and love"*[14] (297).

He acts in response to this "message" and decides to become a carpenter, not in "mere static and hopeful emulation of the Nazarene," but because he assumes that what was good for Christ is good for him. But it would be a serious mistake to say that Faulkner is taking him "all the way." His use of such suggestions of the Christ story is always a way of taking advantage of the ideas best known both to his readers and to the people about whom he is writing.

McCaslin has in any absolute sense failed; his quixotic gesture leads to no genuinely worth-while results. Ike's decision, far from being a positive "penance" for the sins of his fathers, is in the end a demonstration of weakness. Faulkner said of Ike McCaslin, in answer to Cynthia Grenier's query, that repudiation was not enough, was too much a negative gesture:

> Well, I think a man ought to do more than just repudiate. He should have been more affirmative instead of shunning people. (*Accent,* Summer, 1956, p. 175.)

For all its brilliance and its richness of allusion and detail, "The Bear" is not primarily a philosophical piece; nor does it really offer any final statement about its subject. Although Faulkner gives a remarkably complex representation of Ike McCaslin, it would be a serious error to assume, therefore, that he intends Ike to be either a moral spokesman or a sacrificial god. Furthermore, the other sections of *Go Down, Moses* do not support such a contention. *Go Down, Moses* is a many-sided examination of a very difficult and complex problem, the separate details of which (as I have given them above) are presented in "The Bear."

But the real challenge is offered in the figure of Lucas Beauchamp, one of the results of Carothers McCaslin's "sin." His special kind of disposition and his truculent, sullen, and even hostile view of whites are explained in *Go Down, Moses* and dramatized in *Intruder in the Dust*, which is a curious mixture of one of the most successful "adventure narratives" in modern literature (through chapter eight) and the most tortured kind of declamatory rhetoric. Yet the general impression (and this is re-enforced upon rereading) is that everything stated in the later chapters does not really need to be said because it has already been superbly implied in the early ones.

Intruder is, therefore, both an "adventure story"—a murder, a threatened lynching, a lonely and risky trip in the night to a graveyard, a nip-and-tuck race with death, etc.—and a sermon or extended editorial. In the plot, Faulkner has pitted Lucas against the young white boy, Charles Mallison; Lucas challenges Mallison throughout his life to set aside his conventional views of what a Negro is and to treat him as a man instead. From the very first incident when Chick falls into the icy creek and Lucas offers him the hospitality of his home and his food, the contest between the two persists. When Chick offers Lucas money for the "services," Lucas disdains the payment as an insult to his prestige as a man of social position.

> "What's this for?" the man said, not even moving, not even tilting his face downward to look at what was on his palm . . . [Chick watched] his palm turn over not flinging the coins

but spurning them downward ringing onto the bare floor . . ."
(*Intruder*, 15-16).

But Lucas offers the same challenge to the entire community. "He's got to admit he's a nigger," they mutter.[15] In the country store, his insolent calm makes his white neighbors furious with a rage verging on murder. For Chick Mallison, the fury of offended pride does not motivate him as much as an attempt to solve the puzzle of why can he not assert his "masculinity and his white blood" (26). When one of the Gowrie boys is murdered, therefore, the event is enough to make the whites in the town eager to prove Lucas a "nigger"; and the mob gathers before the jail to do its duty and get its revenge. For Mallison, however, the occasion is the final, most crucial stage in the struggle to understand what he as a white must be to Lucas, a Negro.

He is "commissioned" by Lucas to go to the graveyard and prove that Lucas could not have committed the murder. This task is given a sixteen-year-old, as Miss Habersham explains, because "Lucas knew it would take a child—or an old woman like me: someone not concerned with probability, with evidence . . ." (89). In other words, the job requires someone less remote from human facts than a lawyer, or even a sheriff. The mission is undertaken in the night by Mallison, the old lady (a member of the "aristocracy," but "in a plain cotton print dress"), and Chick's Negro companion, Aleck Saunder. This attempt to discover the facts is not because Lucas's danger of being lynched is a "racial outrage," but because it is a "human shame" (97). The adventure has its own complications, and it adds to the shame of the whites—since Gowrie was murdered not by a Negro, but by his brother. It is settled in an atmosphere that sometimes recalls Huckleberry Finn in an incredibly complicated Tom Sawyerish situation. When Lucas is cleared, the men run; rather than admit they were wrong, they flee the shame of their mistake and the outrage of fratricide.

The rest of the book is taken up by Gavin Stevens' rhetorical declamations, which are often supported by moments of extraordinarily fine writing. Irving Howe raises one of the critical issues of *Intruder* when he says: "No novel which has Lucas Beauchamp as a major character can be dismissed as a failure; no novel with Gavin Stevens as its intellectual spokesman can be considered an unqualified success" (*William Faulkner*, 194).[16] A serious question is whether or not Stevens is actually an "intellectual spokesman"; for his is not a flattering portrait and he is only nominally in charge of Lucas's case. The *real* issue of the novel is contained within the struggle of Lucas and Chick to re-evaluate the Negro's status—to go from label and cliché to humanity. Faulkner would certainly be expected to point out the distinction between words and acts; and there are so many words and the acts are undertaken so quietly and with such unostentatious courage that the contrast between the two need not be emphasized.

Stevens is a subject for our next chapter; but it should be stressed that his verbosity overwhelms a set of simple truths in which Faulkner *does* genuinely believe. The novel's first eight chapters beautifully convince us that he does; the book from chapter eight, with the exception of the neatly comic final scene, is editorial bombast and digression containing a succession of cheap metaphors of which only a person whom Faulkner wishes to ridicule can be proud. Stevens is, after all, an "intellectual"; he is a Phi Beta Kappa and has studied at Harvard and at the University of Heidelberg. He has a sense of mission, and he is "on the side of the angels." But he is also, in the several novels in which he appears, a subject alternately of respect and ridicule. Faulkner is saying that the "men of good will," from Horace Benbow on, have erratic careers and often fumble their efforts to maintain moral principles. The last chapters of *Intruder* mark the beginning of Faulkner's own problem, of assuming the risks of overt statement and platform pounding. The publication of *Intruder* was after all only two years before the trip to Stockholm.

CHAPTER 6

The "Eternal Verities"*

I

IN NOVEMBER of 1950 Faulkner was informed that he had been granted the 1949 Nobel Prize for literature. He traveled to Stockholm in the next month to deliver the now famous acceptance address. It was the fourth time an American writer had gained the distinction; but perhaps Faulkner came nearest to earning a unanimous approval from his critics. Cecil B. Williams, after examining much of the press reaction to the event, concluded that

> perhaps it is fair to say that he is the first American author to receive the prize solely on the basis of his contributions to literature as such. The only negative article I found on the Faulkner award, by H. E. Luccock of the Yale Divinity School, did not name a worthier claimant; Luccock based his criticism solely on the ground that Faulkner belonged to a group of modern authors overly-addicted to featuring profanity in their writings.[1]

It is, of course, incorrect to say that the prize changed Faulkner overnight from an unknown to a celebrity; for the task of bringing him to a position of deserved recognition began in 1939 and was greatly aided in 1946 by Cowley's editing of the *Portable Faulkner*. The effect of the prize was

---

* Section one of this chapter and three paragraphs at the end of section three are adapted (with revisions) from my introduction to *Three Decades of Criticism*. I am grateful to the Michigan State University Press for permission to use them.

to bring him "up front," to make a "public man" of him, and to exert such pressure upon the general run of critics and journalists that they could not thereafter dismiss him out of hand so casually as they had in the past. While adverse reactions to Faulkner did not entirely vanish, the prize discouraged some critics and frightened others into confessions of their past errors.

The glaring light of publicity now illuminated Faulkner's status. The obscure and isolated genius who had preferred a Mississippi town of some 4,000 unsophisticated inhabitants to New York and Paris[2] was now at the center of the literary world and had become a public personality. He was called upon to speak his mind on several occasions after the phenomenal success of his Stockholm address. Interviewers now hopefully approached him for comment and reminiscence; he was featured in long and generously illustrated essays in the popular magazines; and he was invited to visit universities as writer in residence or as a guest speaker.

More important than the surprise of public interest in his *succès d'estime* was his willingness to appear, to perform, to speak; he was apparently seriously moved by his eminence, and he endeavored to match the quality of his speech to the unaccustomed virtue of the occasion. No public event, among those succeeding the Stockholm affair, matched in impressive tone the ceremony in the Salle Gaveau, Paris, in May, 1952. As reported by Thelma Smith and Ward Miner (in *Transatlantic Migration*) the event testified to the almost unbelievable prestige Faulkner had achieved in less than two years; the approval was apparently as unequivocal as the period of waiting had been long.

The program went along about as one would expect with sometimes perfunctory or sometimes hearty applause. The one variation from this pattern occurred when Faulkner was introduced by [Denis de] Rougemont. Faulkner stood up; and he had to stand there for several minutes while the audience bravoed, cheered, and gave vent to their enthusiasm in true French fashion. As one French paper described the scene, "The ovation enveloped Faulkner like a tornado—the applause of the single-minded crowd offered him a memorable greeting." And it was this single mindedness that attracted our attention. That audience had come there to see and hear William Faulkner. They had come to the Salle Gaveau that afternoon as an expression of their adulation and almost worship of the writer William Faulkner.[3]

The affair of the Salle Gaveau, as well as others of its kind, was an event of great critical importance, not because of its glamor but because of the rhetoric that preceded and followed it. The truth was that Faulkner had come into a position that demanded of him an unceasing iteration of certain chosen syllables and phrases. These were to echo through the post-Stockholm years in his own writings and in critical appraisals of them. In a sense that has not yet adequately been appreciated, Faulkner himself took the initiative in the criticism of his own work. He was asked to explain to himself and to his admirers the meaning of what he had been saying in the past twenty-five years; and he obliged by providing catch phrases of a very high quality and of a guaranteed somberness of effect. The wonder grew that this man who had described so powerfully and so frequently the ugly, chaotic, miserable, obscene, irrational world of man should have meant all along that he was upholding the "eternal verities" and had, therefore, been without qualification on the side of the angels.

Quite aside from the notoriety of Faulkner's post-Nobel career, let us consider its rhetoric, as featured in the Stockholm Address, in the foreword to the *Faulkner Reader* (1954), in the several interviews with him that have become a critical staple since 1950, in the other speeches he has given, in crucial points in the novels, and conspicuously in the book *Faulkner at Nagano,* edited by Robert A. Jelliffe, which faithfully records his answers to the many questions put to him during his 1955 visit to Japan. The language is an almost incredibly neat succession of devices for accomplishing two ostensible objectives: to explain—perhaps, to explain away—what many critics had called an "unmitigated naturalism" in the description of human affairs; and to act affirmatively in the glare of public acclaim.

Faulkner begins the Stockholm address[4] with an attempt to achieve the first: the phrase "life's work in the agony and sweat of the human spirit" describes both the experience of writing and the experience which is the subject of his fiction. He insists that the intensity of the creative effort must equal the seriousness of the artist's role: the "problems of the human heart in conflict with itself" have been crucially intensified in the atmosphere of World War II. The artist must learn not to be afraid and—I assume—not to yield to deterministic pressures upon his spirit, and not to despair.

The key phrases follow: there should be room in the writer's consciousness for nothing but "the old verities and truths of the heart, the old universal truths lacking which any story is ephemeral and doomed—love and honor and pity and pride and compassion and sacrifice." Faulkner has always used these words in his own writing; they appear as early as *Soldiers' Pay* and they are given both a symbolic and a dramatic setting in Part IV of the famous story "The Bear."[5] But he had never, before 1950, spoken them entirely in his own "voice," except from those of his characters. There is much in these "verities" so nakedly displayed that may suggest a justification of the "agony and sweat" of the earlier fiction; he seems to have wanted either to bring to the light of explicit statement what had earlier "not been clear" or to reassure himself that this is what he had been saying all of the time.

The rest of the speech is affirmation; that is, it is not merely a catalogue of phrases identifying human experience but a rhetorical exercise in assertion and prediction.

> I believe that man will not merely endure: he will prevail. He is immortal, not because he alone among creatures has an inexhaustible voice but because he has a soul, a spirit capable of compassion and sacrifice and endurance. . . . It is [the poet's] privilege to help man endure by lifting his heart, by reminding him of the courage and honor and hope and pride and compassion and pity and sacrifice which have been the glory of his past. . . .

Several characteristics of these words demand scrutiny. They represent a thoroughly secular assertion; that is, they do not appeal either to religious support or to theological sanction, nor do they quote religious documents. Faulkner makes an important distinction between the heart and the glands; he seems anxious to judge morally the difference between an organ of life and the means of excitation to pleasure and indulgence. To Faulkner's basic humanist distinction are added the necessary sentimentalities of whatever "the heart" has come to mean in normal unthinking discourse. The point is that Faulkner is trying here to find a way out of the "naturalist impasse" to which some critics of his earlier work had consigned him.

Furthermore, the rhetoric of his address reveals an overpowering desire to articulate directly the hundreds of complex truths of "the human heart" which remain in a tenuous and ambiguous state of suspension in his novels. To bring them into the light of ceremonial day is to clear them of all circumstance of doubt and obscurity. The rhetoric is overt, forcefully direct, entirely unclear (as an instrument of understanding literature, at least), and powerfully effective. It gave the impression of changing Faulkner overnight from a "naturalistic monster" to a "moral hero" in popular contemporary reviews.[6]

II

Obviously, the "eternal verities" of which Faulkner spoke and wrote in the 1950's require a strong, firm spokesman. They were not "new ideas" to him, for they are present, implicitly at least, from the beginning. The difference is not a "change of heart," but one of method. Robert Penn Warren spoke in 1946 of the "voice" of Faulkner as playing a role in his style—as "a method in which the medium is ultimately a 'voice' as index to sensibility."[7] Warren obviously referred then to a matter of technique rather than of ideas; but the "voice" of Faulkner seems worthy of study because it suggests his growing desire for a more clearly understood assertion. That is, it has gradually become more fully a means of controlling his statement and expressing his intention.

The question of the "voice" and its growing strength is especially relevant to the role of Gavin Stevens—a character by no means unambiguous—in the fiction of the 1950's. Faulkner's treatment on occasion suggests a major role for him; but at other times he is represented as vulnerable—even more than slightly ridiculous. Beginning with chapter eight of *Intruder*, he gradually takes over the novel and delivers its "message." But we already have the assurance that the main direction of the novel is in other hands; and, in the light of Stevens's having had to yield in the crucial responsibilities of the novel to women and children, his status is much in doubt since he begins to orate ostensibly for Mallison's benefit.

Almost the same thing may be said for his participation in *The Town* and in *The Mansion*: most of the time we assume that "his heart is in the right place" and that he watches zealously over the distribution of good and evil in the moral economy of Jefferson. Yet he is presented as fallible, often as not terribly effective, and sometimes as a bit obtuse. Faulkner has surely had his reservations about Stevens's ultimate effectiveness as a "good strong hero." To Cynthia Grenier he said that Stevens "was a good man but he didn't succeed in living up to his ideal. But his nephew, the boy [Chick Mallison], I think he may grow up to be a better man than his uncle. I think he may succeed as a human being" (*Accent*, Summer, 1956, p. 175).

Faulkner's sense of the affirmative hero has become a challenge to his readers and a set of demands upon them. Remarks that he has made to students and interviewers suggest that he is scrutinizing more and more narrowly the behavior of his past heroes. Having once created them, he has seemingly put them "on their own"; they have to prove themselves. "There seem to be three stages," he said at Virginia, *à propos* of heroic positions:

. . . The first says, This is rotten, I'll have no part of it, I will take death first. The second says, this is rotten, I don't like it, I can't do anything about it, but at least I will not participate in it myself, I will go into a cave or climb a pillar to sit on. The third says, this stinks and I'm going to do something about it . . . (*Faulkner in the University*, 245-46).

He seems in this statement to be reviewing his own fiction from a post-Nobel point of view. The first of these heroes is obviously represented in the suicides of Bayard Sartoris and Quentin Compson. Faulkner singles out Ike McCaslin as an example of the second. As for the third, there are many candidates: Gavin Stevens surely, although he more often than not falls short; Mallison, who represents frequently the kind of sense Faulkner admires in the above remark; perhaps Ratliff, with his ingenious capacity for good; and the corporal of *A Fable*.

Requiem for a Nun appears to be Gavin Stevens's most generous opportunity to "make good" as a latter-day Faulkner hero. In it, Stevens is not only a lawyer out to see that justice is done (as he had been in *Intruder* and *Knight's Gambit*); he is a moralist, climbing what he calls "the symbolical hill" toward the truth and urging and persuading Temple Drake to admit her complicity in the assorted evils of *Sanctuary*. Mrs. Vickery has well stated the difference between the Stevens of *Intruder* and that of *Requiem*. In the latter, Stevens, though he is still garrulous and too fond of the rhetoric of moral pronouncements, "is no longer content with words as an end product." He has also "curbed his tendency to be both judge and jury." Now he is anxious to bring Temple Drake's sense of guilt to the surface and to conduct her on the long journey toward redemption. "Unlike Benbow, his exploration is not *for* but *with* people; condescension is replaced by ministration. In a sense, he willingly destroys his own office and function—the lawyer is supplanted by the attendant priest whose duty is to guide not judge."[8]

Requiem resumes the events of *Sanctuary* but brings a radically new perspective upon them—so radically new that several facts of the earlier novel fall by the wayside. Some eight years after those incidents, Temple has agreed to marry Gowan Stevens, who had earlier deserted her on the road to Popeye and ruin; and they return to Jefferson from Paris. But Temple is still secretly in love with her Memphis past, and it is re-established through the sudden appearance of a young brother of her lover of *Sanctuary*. She agrees to desert her new ménage to go with him, but their plans are thwarted by Nancy Mannigoe, the "nun" of *Requiem*,[9] who smothers Temple's baby to force her to see her moral responsibility.

Gavin Stevens's task is not only to explain Nancy's reasons for the murder but to draw Temple into awareness and open admission of guilt. His effort is presented in a three-act play, which is detachable from the novel and has, in fact, been twice detached from it.[10] In act one, Nancy is sentenced to die; she had been defended by Gavin Stevens, who now turns to Temple and Gowan for help in an attempt to intercede with the Governor. At 2:00 A.M., in the Governor's office (Act Two), he listens to Gowan's speeches about the moral law; but while Temple is making her confession, Gavin replaces the Governor, and it is to him that Temple tells all.

Act three occurs in the Jefferson jail. Nancy, who awaits her death with serenity, lectures Temple on the consolations of religion. But Temple leaves the jail unconvinced; for she is uncertain about the God Nancy invokes:

> What about me? Even if there is [a heaven] and somebody waiting in it to forgive me, there's still tomorrow and tomorrow. And suppose tomorrow and then nobody there, nobody waiting to forgive me—
> Nancy: Believe.
> Temple: Believe what, Nancy? Tell me.
> Nancy: Believe.[11]

Nancy believes, without assurances. Temple, however, leaves the jail with a sense of foreboding and damnation:

Anyone to save it. Anyone who wants it. If there is none, I'm
sunk. We all are. Doomed. Damned.
    Stevens: Of course we are. Hasn't He been telling us that
for going on two thousand years? (*Requiem,* 286.)

Gavin Stevens has clearly counseled an admission of guilt
without a precise assurance of either God or heaven. Faulkner
is not suggesting here the absence of either one; he is fighting
the easy assumption that we, as human souls, do not need
to act morally on our own. God's message to us is that we are
doomed, but this means that the challenge is to our own
limited but nevertheless strong powers of "enduring" and
"prevailing." He wants, as he said at the University of Virginia,
"some conception of God," call Him what man will. In this
connection, he suggested that the work of Camus (whose
thinking, he suspects, requires a God) will long outlast that
of Jean-Paul Sartre. (*Faulkner in the University,* 161.)

The drama of *Requiem* alternates with long prose passages
which give a type of "history" of Jefferson and provide a background for the dramatic exchanges. They are, however, more
interesting for what they suggest of a continuing line of discourse or commentary. They are a continuation of *Go Down,
Moses,* in their reflections upon the land; they also comment
at length upon the "legend," which Malcolm Cowley had
summarized in his introduction to the *Portable;* and, finally,
they communicate a sense of tradition, linking the Jefferson
present with its past in gossip and legend—even on occasions,
its "geological past." Echoes of *Sanctuary,* of course, and also
of *The Hamlet* are present. In general, the Jefferson setting
is given both depth and breadth—moved back and forth in
time—for the purpose of supporting and augmenting the argument of "the play."

What is that argument? First of all, there is a humanist
appeal to moral responsibilities. Nancy Mannigoe's simple
statement, "I believe" (in what, she is not quite sure) suggests at least two notes: that true belief defies and transcends
analysis and skepticism, and that it is a "secular belief." That
is, Faulkner would agree with the existentialist that to depend

too much and too easily on *any* external protection or security is "bad faith," or an act of self-deception. But he is trying to construct the basis of belief in terms of a purely human, limited self-knowledge. To acknowledge one's guilt as the beginning of the recognition of one's moral strength seems to be the message of Gavin Stevens's earnest and prolonged accounting of his legal and moral stewardship. In acquitting himself of it, he is presented apparently with much approval, and he quite obviously takes a role of such urgent assertion (and frequently with a humility not present in *Intruder* and elsewhere) that he attracts attention outside himself as character. Faulkner's last *ex cathedra* statements seem to involve a test of his characters as persons independent of context, as though he were passing judgment upon their success or failure in coming up to his standards.

Requiem, then, argues a secular faith which uses the Christian metaphors without committing either characters or readers to accepting them as literally true. But, despite this, Faulkner seems to be saying that they must be persuasively and convincingly strong guides to the proper adherence to human responsibilities. The elaborate structure of *A Fable* testifies to his trust in the strength and vividness of these metaphors.

III

The idea of *A Fable* came to Faulkner, he says, shortly after Pearl Harbor in 1942. Suppose, he thought, the unknown soldier were "Christ again, under that fine big cenotaph with the eternal flame burning on it? . . ." (*Faulkner in the University*, 27.) Such a use of the Christ figure in modern literature is scarcely unusual; many novels have suggested or explicitly introduced Christ as a common, "unknown" soldier in World War I. Faulkner, however, develops the suggested analogy more elaborately and exhaustively than any of his contemporaries.

The illiterate French corporal who leads the mutiny in *A Fable* is an adaptation of the Christ and his twelve followers are like the twelve apostles. One of them betrays him; another denies him three times. The corporal is tempted by the Supreme Commander of the Allied armies, as Christ was tempted by Satan. He is killed by a firing squad; and, when he falls, his head is caught in barbed wire—the modern equivalent of the crown of thorns.

All these parallels are designed to bring the full force of the Christ story to bear upon Faulkner's text; but it is a secular text, just as the corporal is a secular Christ. The text, often stated in the novel but repeated near the end by the old general is that man will not only "endure," but will "prevail" after "the last ding dong of doom has rung and died. . . ."[12] This statement does not mean that man is "saved" because he has the "power of grace" within him. Simply, it indicates that, being human, he is capable of goodness and that the balance is, therefore, in favor of his survival—of his "prevailing" beyond the terrors of cosmic or of man-made annihilation.

We can then say that the "allegory" of *A Fable* is not so important as the fact that the Christ story provides a frame in which the strength of men may be dramatized. Man is "as if" he were a Christ; he does not depend upon a god-given power to act or to suffer: he does both on his own initiative. The meaning of all suggestive uses of the Christ parallel in Faulkner's work[13] is, therefore, clear: the Christ story is used as a metaphor to strengthen the human story. The title of *A Fable* is very important in directing the reader concerning the way in which he should read the novel: it *is* a fable of the human condition. But it should also be said that Christ's story—and the corporal's adaptation of it—is necessary to Faulkner to lend strength and to give sanction to man's struggle. Without it, man may not realize his power to endure and prevail, and may therefore not use it. In a very real sense, Faulkner intended *A Fable* to dramatize and "prove" his assertions in the Stockholm address.

Several additional comments about *A Fable* may prove useful. Faulkner's choice of World War I is perhaps not a difficult problem in view of his own knowledge of it and of his admission that he started to work on *A Fable* in 1942. But it is also probable that the trench warfare of World War I was the most appropriate locale of his action. As Andrew Lytle has said, "The four-year stalemate not only returns man to the mud and slime; it imposes the condition of the earthworm, one of the lowest and blindest forms of life."[14] In these circumstances, the elements of man are reduced to their lowest possible condition and a basic conflict is set up between the necessities of order and the state of innocence. The degradation of the trench, the imposed order of the battlefield: these are a paradigm of all forms of order and innocence, the jail, the wasteland of the war, the drives of the self.

War is, therefore, a heightened symbol on one hand of man's greeds and weaknesses, and on the other of the level of necessary action. War, a situation most extremely opposed to innocence, exerts the strongest pressure upon man's will to endure. But it is also a false ordering of the society of man; it therefore encourages mutiny, rebellion, and gestures of a return to a state of innocence. Underlying the surface of *A Fable*, however, there is a strong, and even a desperate feeling that man must reassert his "innocence"—or that Faulkner hopes he will despite the fact that man's positive acts are almost always doomed to failure.

This move forward in the Faulkner world is more than half met by a step backward. Evil stains the good; knowledge, fear, and greed pervert innocence. There is, therefore, a constant tendency to make assertions about man's nature and destiny beyond the point that the conditions seem to warrant. There is also a tendency to make assertion stand for truth because it *must*. This urgent sense of mission rather vaguely resembles the quality of Edwin Arlington Robinson's assertions "in the face of contrary evidence." Faulkner's hero is the "man against the sky," who wills a triumph over naturalist threats of doom and annihilation. He acts as he does out of reserves of self-belief and confidence; he says, with Nancy Mannigoe of *Requiem*, "I don't know. But I believes" (281).

The real quarrel with *A Fable* lies not with its being more "positive" than "negative," but with its degree of intellectual maturity. Philip Blair Rice, late professor of philosophy at Kenyon College, accused the novel of intellectual failure:

> That he has failed to find adequate incidents, agonists and symbols to realize [the Nobel speech] dramatically and poetically is a conviction that grows steadily and painfully upon the reader; that he has failed to dominate the intellectual problems with which he has been struggling—for the book cannot be taken as other than an effort at something like a social, a theological, a philosophical novel—is quite as evident.[15]

Very few other criticisms of *A Fable* failed to mention the problem of intellectual failure—of the failure to match conception with presentation. Catholic critic Ernest Sandeen stressed the very real theological difficulties attendant upon the reduction of Christ to secular levels:

> The source of these difficulties lies in the associations made between Christ and the character, the corporal. Because of the many superficial resemblances drawn between the two, the corporal by implication becomes an interpretation of Christ. . . . [The parallel] perversely attributes a gnostic or manichaean outlook to Christ and at the same time an incarnational outlook to the Church. . . .[16]

The difficulty becomes one of credibility. To return to Christ after having strayed from virtue is an act acceptable to both God and man in a time when Christ is invested with divinity and humanity. If it is not possible to accept such a fusion of powers, the center of moral conflict becomes man, a hero, in whom good and evil create Manichaean tensions not easily resolved by an act of the will.

The obscurity of the Nobel Prize address once more afflicts the reader and critic. That man will endure and prevail because he has survived his self-imposed agonies is an affirmation difficult to maintain and to dramatize. One is left simply with the strong conviction of Faulkner, who has elsewhere abundantly proved himself aware of the moral contradictions in man but asserts that he will, nevertheless, endure and prevail over their disastrous results. Whatever the consequences of our having thus been cut adrift from Christian essentials, the attempt has been made in *A Fable* to write a Christian allegory that lacks at least one of its Christian co-ordinates. Perhaps, as Dayton Kohler suggests, "Faulkner's treatment of Hebraic-Christian myth is like Joyce's use of the Homeric story in *Ulysses* and Mann's adaptation of Faustian legend in *Doctor Faustus*."[17] But there is some doubt that the literary responsibilities of the older to the modern text in these other two cases are nearly so exacting; nor is the hero of either so necessitously linked to doctrinal demands.

IV

When Faulkner died of a heart attack, July 6, 1962, he left a final novel published just a few weeks before, *The Reivers.* He had told Jean Stein in 1956 that "my last book will be the Doomsday Book, the Golden Book, of Yoknapatawpha County. Then I shall break the pencil and I'll have to stop" (*Three Decades,* 82). It is obvious, however, that *The Reivers* was not intended to be that "Golden Book," as well as that death forced him to quit before he was satisfied he had completed the story of the County. In fact, the novel is a secondary "grace note" on the lives of County people, an adventure story that has reflections of the young boy's initiation into the ways of the world, a comedy with sentimental overtones.

Everything that needs to be said has already been said about *The Reivers.* Cleanth Brooks tries hardest to give the book significance in *William Faulkner* (349-68). The principal truth about the novel is that it clearly demonstrates the inexhaustible resources of the County for Faulkner's imagination. There is no evidence, therefore, that he would not have gone on, had he lived, producing more novels and short stories, availing himself of the world his fertile imagination had so richly endowed. Critics have pointed to the quality of cross-reference in *The Reivers:* Miss Reba's brothel, from *Sanctuary;* Boon Hogganbeck, from "The Bear"; the Priests, a

part of the legitimate branch of the prolific McCaslin family.[18]
Above all, there is the theme, frequently used in Faulkner's
work, of the young boy's initiation into a world in which good
and evil must be discriminated. In "The Bear," this initiation
ceremony is linked to forms of folk ritual and myth. In
Intruder in the Dust, Chick Mallison's voyage to understanding is closely tied to the white-Negro relationships and the
moral issues they raise. Here, in *The Reivers*, the experience
of eleven-year-old Lucius Priest (he is describing it many
years later to his grandson) seems to take on the appearance
of an education in manners, in what a "gentleman" and a
"lady" should know.

Despite the boy's encounters with violence, meanness, and
chicanery, *The Reivers* has a mellow and even a sentimental
quality; the world it defines has precise answers to moral
questions, and the answers frequently depend on the "gentleman's code." The "adventure" with which it is concerned
begins with the "borrowing" of an automobile, itself a status
symbol of a curious sort (since it was bought by "Boss"
Priest because Colonel Sartoris had put through a city ordi-
nance forbidding the ownership of such vehicles). The car
in this case is wholly without symbolic malice; Faulkner has
rarely treated machinery with so humorous a tenderness.
When Lucius' maternal grandmother dies, the parents and
grandparents leave for four to ten days. The temptation is too
great. Boon Hogganbeck determines upon a trip in the automobile, to Memphis and Miss Reba's, especially to his favorite
prostitute, Miss Corrie.

The rest is a mixture of comical enterprises and incidents
and the education of Lucius in the moral variegations of the
adult world. Several petty villains enter the piece, notably
Otis, a relative of Miss Corrie, and Butch, a deputy sheriff.
But there are also small heroics and dignity. As the adventure
plays itself out, we are left with the rather dubious suggestion
that an eleven-year-old, as a consequence of his having been
exposed to ("pushed into") a variety of situations, has incredibly "matured." There are half-comical and half-violent, but

quite successfully muted, notions that he has "grown up" into the adult world. Quite aside from the doubt that this *is* an adult world into which Lucius is introduced, there is the quality of "reminiscence" which affects the novel's tone (the novel's subtitle is *A Reminiscence*). Brooks says of it that Faulkner was "successful in his handling the tone of this novel, casting over Yoknapatawpha County and its inhabitants a kind of golden retrospective atmosphere" (*William Faulkner,* 351).

It is true that Lucius has the opportunity to see much "adult behavior," some of it perhaps edifying. He is also aware of what is right and what is wrong, but he sometimes has difficulty in applying his beliefs to local situations. The reform of Miss Corrie (whose real name is Everbe Corinthia) may be considered "exemplary," and surely Lucius plays the good knight's role for her at least once; but she plays false to her vow, when it proves expedient to do so, and Lucius is more than nonplussed by her act. In any case, he is supposed to have "become a man" as a consequence of the adventures of Memphis and Parsham. His grandfather, who had stepped in, in place of the father, to lecture Lucius instead of whipping him, advises acceptance—living with the knowledge of his wrongdoing:

> "Live with it? You mean, forever? For the rest of my life? Not ever to get rid of it? Never? I cant. Dont you see I cant?"
>
> "Yes you can," he said. "You will. A gentleman can live through anything. He faces anything. A gentleman accepts the responsibility of his actions and bears the burden of their consequences, even when he did not himself instigate them but only acquiesced to them, didn't say No though he knew he should. . . ."[19]

CHAPTER 7

The Legacy of Faulkner

I

THE REIVERS can be said to have closed Faulkner's career with, at best, a semi-colon. That it happened to be the last novel he published before his death was an accident of fate and has nothing to do with the total realization of his work. Aside from its comedy, and even to an extent in terms of it, *The Reivers* borrows its grace and interest from the fact that before it some eighteen[1] novels were published, all but five of which were devoted to the enrichment and vivid actualization of Yoknapatawpha County.

That County is his major legacy. Of the five novels that do not deal directly with it, two are post-World War I "apprenticeship" novels, one (*Pylon*) has a limited value, one exists on the "edge" of Yoknapatawpha (*The Wild Palms*, in which the prison at Parchman links it to several scenes in Yoknapatawpha novels, like *The Mansion*), and one (*A Fable*) is lifted entirely out of the scene of man and uses him primarily in terms of moral and religious allegory. These books, of course, have their merits, and there is no doubt that they need to be examined carefully before a final assessment of Faulkner can be made. But with the opportunity we now have to look back upon the completed work,[2] it is the great achievement, from 1929 to 1962, of the County that excites. I should like to consider this achievement under three headings: its scope and variety; Faulkner's association with it; and the fluctuations of value and tone attributed to it.

II

As for the first of these, the reader will surely marvel at the growth of the County, in scope and depth. There are now at least four glossaries, or dictionaries, or who's who's, of the Yoknapatawpha County folk, who in 1936 numbered some 15,611.[3] This number is, of course, misleading, since Faulkner worked mostly in depth, and with time and family patterns, so that the dead from the past often play a more powerful role than their living heirs. The surprising fact is that the more complicated the map of the County became (as more and more persons were named and "individuated"), the more complex was its meaning. Faulkner's two great talents were his ability to bring these figures to life as individual creatures and his remarkable power of bringing them into relationships (blood, emotional, political, etc.) with each other. There is no doubt that these talents are partly the result of the fact that Faulkner did have living models, as well as his experience in *hearing about* his family and the families of others in Oxford. So that, when (as he says, in response to Sherwood Anderson's advice), he gave up trying to imitate contemporaries or writers of the recent past, and settled in Jefferson, he already had an amazing reservoir of facts and personages to draw upon.

A look at the families he created and defined in terms of family and social relationships will convince one of the "infinite variety" he has communicated in his imaginary world.[4] Aside from the Indians and Negroes of the early nineteenth century (of both of whom Sam Fathers of "The Bear" is a descendant), there are twelve major families in the County: Habersham, Holston, Grenier, Benbow, Stevens, Sartoris, Compson, McCaslin-Edmonds, Priest, Sutpen, McCallum, and Snopes. Of course, these vary immensely in size and station. There are a great many examples of "crossing over" and of rises and declines in the century and a half of time in which Faulkner places them. Even Flem Snopes gains (plots for) "respectability" in Jefferson before his cousin Mink murders him.

The first Habersham (Doctor Samuel) came to the County about 1800, with Alexander Holston and Louis Grenier. One of Habersham's descendants, Eunice, a seventy-year-old spinster, plays a prominent role in *Intruder in the Dust*, more than a century after the original Habersham appeared in the County. Holston set up the Holston House, which figures prominently in several works, noticeably in *Absalom, Absalom!* The Grenier family seems to have declined after the first generation: in 1905, over a century after Louis Grenier arrived, a Dan Grinnup appears (in *The Reivers*). It was Grenier's plantation, known as "Old Frenchman's Place" in the 1890's, that was given to Flem Snopes (in *The Hamlet*), to be traded later to V. K. Ratliff, Homer Bookwright, and Henry Armstid, in Snopes's most successful hoax.

Of the Benbows, the most important, of course, is Horace (though Narcissa plays a fairly important role in *Sartoris*), whose attempts to free Goodwin (in *Sanctuary*) are entirely disappointed. The other Benbows have only brief mentions. Of the Stevenses, who play prominent roles, Judge Stevens is mentioned in *Requiem for a Nun* (whose inter-chapters are a compendium of Yoknapatawpha facts) as mayor of Jefferson at the age of eighty. Gavin is, of course, the most important member of the family. He first appears in *Light in August*, and he is an important character in *Intruder, Requiem, The Town* and *The Mansion*.

It is interesting that almost all of the persons on whom Faulkner depends for major positions in the later novels come from pioneer families who become "aristocratic" leaders of the community. Gavin Stevens obviously inherits many of his convictions, but he is also a proud man, with all the badges of distinction (Harvard, Heidelberg, Phi Beta Kappa, etc.). The Sartorises often seem to come closest to resembling the family and the descendants of Colonel William Cuthbert Falkner.[5] The resemblance is surely not exact; Faulkner does not permit anyone autobiographical license. The very first

Yoknapatawpha novel (*Sartoris*, antedating the appearance of *The Sound and the Fury* by some six months) is of course central to the Sartoris story; *The Unvanquished* features the Sartoris past and especially the Civil War. In *Light in August* Colonel Sartoris is noted as having shot two members of the Burden family, whose descendant Joanna lives on the outskirts of Jefferson and is killed by Joe Christmas.

The Compson family, of course, is at the center of *The Sound and the Fury*, and in the Appendix to that novel (which Faulkner called the "fifth writing of the story"[6]). The scope of the Compson decline can be seem in the contrast between Jason I (Jason Lycurgus Compson), who in 1813 traded a racing horse to Ikkemotubbe for a square mile of land, the "Compson Estate," and Jason IV, "the first sane Compson since before Culloden and (a childless bachelor) hence the last...."[7] Jason Richmond Compson, father of Quentin, Caddy, Benjy, and Jason IV, is a later revelation of the decline; he has married Caroline Bascomb (who becomes a "non-mother" to her children), and with his brother-in-law Maury drinks and talks his life away.

There is almost always a sense of erosion in the histories of the prominent families recorded in the Yoknapatawpha saga. The Sartoris family all but ends in the violent deaths of the two Bayards; the Compsons all but disappear as a result of suicide, drink, and castration. Only the bastard child of Caddy's affairs in 1909 remains. She disappeared in 1928 with a carnival man whose name is not mentioned. Caddy herself is last seen in the company of a Nazi general during the occupation of Paris. The McCaslin-Edmonds family in a sense thrives, but that is because there are two branches of it, the more prolific of which comes from the bar sinister, the generations of children born from the act of miscegenation. As in the case of the Sutpen family of *Absalom, Absalom!*, the McCaslins suffer from the "sin" and the urgent sense of the need to "atone" for it. An examination of the McCaslin genealogy (as in Volpe, *Reader's Guide*, [231]) shows that the descendants of Lucius Quintus Carothers McCaslin (1772-1837) number seventeen whites distributed through seven generations, and seventeen Negroes or persons with some Negro blood in six generations.

The Snopeses are the product of a very different kind of moral defection. The proliferation of Snopeses in the County comes from the twin occasions of opportunism and opportunity. Through the most elaborate and ingenious kinds of chicanery noted in American fiction, the Snopeses steadily increase their number, until the most cunning of them have become bankers and petty politicians. The range of Snopes character and type is seen in the Snopes names that come down from the first-noted of them, Ab of Civil War bushwacker times (*The Unvanquished*): Admiral Dewey Snopes, Bilbo Snopes, Byron Snopes, Launcelot (Lump) Snopes, Mink Snopes, Montgomery Ward Snopes, Orestes Snopes, Wallstreet Panic Snopes, Watkins Products Snopes, *et al.*[8]

III

As the numbers of County personalities increased through the years, as the map and the genealogies filled in, Faulkner became more and more involved with them; they were never merely "imaginary," nor did they necessarily simply add with the years. The peculiarities of Faulkner's relationship to these creatures can be seen both in his preoccupation with them and in his role in making them articulate. In regard to the first of these, Faulkner was, like Balzac, involved in an almost personal relationship, so that the life of his imagination became more real than the life around him. For many years, he said nothing about his work ("I ain't a literary man" was his usual reply to queries about his work). After the Nobel Prize, he became increasingly articulate, almost entirely about the Yoknapatawpha world. Every moral and philosophical observation he made about the human condition seemed either to come directly out of the fictional world or to anticipate a development in it.

This immersion in his own private world is especially obvious in the books and articles and in interviews he allowed after 1950. The best of these, *Faulkner in the University*, admirably demonstrates the quality of his commitment. He was not especially good with questions about his craft, and seemed uneasy when asked them; but he responded quickly and with a sense of easy familiarity to queries about persons in his County. He knew them with a sense of great intimacy; they came quickly to mind as soon as their names were mentioned.

Another aspect of this "proprietorship" can be noted in Faulkner's maneuvering his characters from novel to story to novel and from decade to decade. Any dictionary of his characters will give the simple facts of this practice and indicate the amazing intricacies of it. There are any number of examples. Jewel, of *As I Lay Dying* (1930), is discovered as having bought a horse in the sale of Texas ponies described in *The Hamlet* (1940). The Sartorises range widely, from their first published appearance (1929) back to the days just after the Civil War, when a Sartoris takes over in the campaign against Northern whites (the "Burdens") (*Light in August*, 1932). Though both senior and junior Bayards die in *Sartoris*, they still remain alive in Faulkner's imagination, which moves backward and forward in time and thus re-animates almost every character who might have been "killed off."

In many ways, Faulkner, in his management of his creatures, treats them both "horizontally" and "vertically." That is, he gives a view in breadth of the disposition of his world at any one given time; but his maneuvering of time, one of his most distinguished contributions to modern fiction,[9] causes his characters to remain "alive" at all times, whether in actuality (when the narrative moves backward in time to pick them up), or in memory (as at the beginning of chapter two of *Absalom, Absalom!*, when ". . . the listening, the hearing in 1909 mostly about that which he already knew, since he had been born in and still breathed the same air in which the church bells had rung in 1833 . . ."[10]).

There are many meanings in these complications. For example, the difference in time of publication between *Sanc-*

tuary and *Requiem for a Nun* is some twenty years; the actual (or imaginary, if you will) difference between the *settings* of the novels is considerably less, some eight years, or about one-third of the time. This is a case in which the publication dates are far more important than the chronological differences. In twenty years, Faulkner had considerably altered his moral view of the Temple Drake incident. He had always professed to be "ashamed" of the novel,[11] but the major reason for the changes was his felt need, after the Nobel Award, for an articulate, courageous, morally determined person, which led to his picking up the Gavin Stevens of 1932 (where he appears briefly in *Light in August*) and refurbishing him, so that he becomes a very loud spokesman indeed, a knight in business suit and with the Phi Beta Kappa status symbol dangling from his vest as he climbs that "symbolical hill."

In order to make such changes in his moral view obvious and operational, Faulkner had to deal rather harshly with the creatures who had served him in earlier publications. The "mistakes" made by creators always mystify the descendants of their Adams. Faulkner's moral views both hardened and were given a more strident, open rhetoric. Many critics have complained about this quality of the fiction beginning in 1948, the material after chapter eight of *Intruder*. I do not think that speculation about the reasons for this change is especially fruitful, though the post-1950 Faulkner is radically different from the man who wrote the novels through chapter eight of *Intruder*.

Thus, his new attitude toward Yoknapatawpha is almost contemporaneous with the great public recognition he received from 1950 to his death in 1962. I do not wish to suggest that the ideas and their accompanying rhetoric were newly and suddenly born; it is just that Faulkner became more and more unhappy about the manner in which he had expressed them. Any number of urgencies served to exert pressure upon him to be more explicit, to preach, to endow his characters with superficial badges of intellectual and moral competence.

IV

The "voice" of Faulkner, of which Sister Kristin Morrison speaks so intelligently,[12] is a very complex instrument. Much of the way, it is used to help his characters speak who might otherwise be incapable of articulating their responses, or even of *narrating* them. Benjy of *The Sound and the Fury*, for example, would not have been able to *say anything*, and pages 23-94 of that novel[13] would have had to be blank. The "voice" is rarely called upon to provide *that* much of a novel's substance. In mid-career, Faulkner employed the "voice" brilliantly, with the aim of raising not the moral tone of his characters, but their power of "meaning" the most that their personalities and the implications of their being can command.

There are any number of examples. The "truth" for the Faulkner of 1929 to 1950 is for the most part, not something shining in neon lights on the curve of the freeway that leads into Glendale,[14] but a complex matter that varies for every consciousness that apprehends it.[15] Faulkner was aware of several levels of response. People who could scarcely sign their names were tortured by complex fears and desires. The "voice" brings brilliantly to the reader's consciousness what a person *genuinely* is, as distinguished from what he is able to say, the point of view he is able to articulate.[16]

These facts can be illustrated any number of times. Faulkner, for a time at least, broke through the Jamesian barrier, the idea that one had to have a "beautiful intelligence" in order to represent significant moral facts. He ignored the Jamesian caution, yet, because of his rhetorical brilliance, was able to communicate, not *his* views, but those of his characters.[17]

The changes in Faulkner's last twelve years were not only a matter of his moving from the private craftsman to the public spokesman (the preacher, the editorialist, the man who wished to "teach" the young generation), but also a matter of his insistent desire to make his characters *speak for him*. The Corporal of *A Fable* could not have said one percent of what he means; there is little or no *rapport* between Faulkner and his creature. The rhetoric intervenes; no one can accept *any* of the persons in *A Fable* as *persons*. The same criticism may be visited upon *Requiem;* and *The Town* and *The Mansion* have taken the spirit of *The Hamlet* beyond any real conclusion concerning the meaning of Flem Snopes. The humanity (or anti-humanity; in any case, the man beneath the skin) is occasionally revealed in the second and third volume of the trilogy.

It is futile (or captious) to take issue with an artist of such great skill simply because he cannot rhetorically keep pace with his convictions and beliefs. We should be eternally grateful that Yoknapatawpha exists, and has been elaborated. We can see in it (whether we are Northerners or Southerners) the image both of our fears and of our hates. The obsessive, agonized behavior of a Mink Snopes is not very different from the quieter concerns of all of us. Faulkner has illuminated, illustrated, dramatized, and interpreted the basic issues of our time. The paradox of our frustrations and our futile rationalizations concerning them ("I'm white; the Negroes are evil, or weak, or imbecilic, etc.") must be examined by an artist who, quite without involving himself in the superficies of the problem, has deep sense of the human condition; who, despite his sensitivity to the color of skins, has tried to dramatize the moral issues in terms of the human beings who are immediately involved in them.

Notes and References

Notes and References

1. At the University of Virginia, Faulkner said it should be pronounced Yok-na-pa-TAW-pha, and that it was a Chickasaw Indian word meaning "water runs slow through flat land." See *Faulkner in the University* (Charlottesville, Va., 1959), p. 74.

2. Quoted in William Van O'Connor, *The Tangled Fire of William Faulkner* (Minneapolis, 1954), p. 18.

3. Rutgers University Press, 1958. There are also short sketches from the Jan.-Feb. issue of *The Double Dealer*.

4. See his remarks to Cynthia Grenier, in *Accent*, XVI (Summer, 1956), 172: "*As I Lay Dying* took me just about six weeks. . . . Just came like that. I just thought of all the natural catastrophes that could happen to a family and let them all happen. . . ."

5. In addition to these titles in the 1930's, Faulkner published another volume of poems (*A Green Bough*, 1933), and two collections of short stories (*These Thirteen*, 1931, and *Dr. Martino*, 1934). His *Collected Stories*, which appeared in 1950, is in itself worthy of a full-length study. I shall, however, refer to it only in connection with the novels, which are after all his major achievements.

6. In *Writers at Work*, edited by Malcolm Cowley (New York: Viking Press, 1958), p. 141. Also in *William Faulkner: Three Decades of Criticism*, edited by Frederick J. Hoffman and Olga W. Vickery (East Lansing, Mich., 1960), pp. 81-82. Hereafter this book will be referred to in the text as *Three Decades*.

7. The modern spelling of Faulkner appeared in his first publication, *The Marble Faun*. From 1919 to 1924, Faulkner spelled his name two ways, with "u" and without "u." After 1924, the "u" seemed fated to remain.

8. "The Faulkners: Recollections of a Gifted Family," in *Three Decades*, pp. 62-63. Cantwell's essay was first published in *New World Writing*, Number 2 (1952).

9. *William Faulkner: A Critical Study* (New York: Random House, 1952), p. 8. The statement, somewhat revised, is on p. 9 of Howe's new edition (New York: Vintage, 1962).

10. *Go Down, Moses* (New York: Modern Library, 1955), p. 193; originally published, New York: Random House, 1942. Hereafter referred to in text as *Moses*.

11. *PMLA*, LXXXI (June, 1956), 299-300.

12. For a valuable study of the figure in nineteenth-century American literature, see R. W. B. Lewis's *The American Adam* (Chicago: University of Chicago Press, 1955). See also Philip Young's *Hemingway* (New York: Rinehart, 1952) and Frederick J. Hoffman in the *Virginia Quarterly Review* (Spring 1961).

13. New York: Random House, 1948, p. 147. Hereafter referred to as *Intruder*.

14. New York: Modern Library, 1946, p. 195. Originally published, New York: Jonathan Cape and Harrison Smith, 1929. Hereafter referred to in text as *SF*.

15. *Light in August* (New York: Modern Library, 1950), p. 431. Originally published, Harrison Smith and Robert Haas, 1932. Hereafter referred to in text as *LA*.

16. *Sanctuary* (New York: Modern Library, 1932), p. 2. Originally published, New York: Cape and Smith, 1931. With the exception of an Introduction by Faulkner to the Modern Library edition, the two editions are identical and obviously printed from the same plates.

17. *Modern Fiction Studies*, II (Autumn, 1956), 144.

18. For a useful discussion of this point, see Robert Penn Warren's essay, in *Three Decades*, pp. 109-24. See also Sister Kristin Morrison, "Faulkner's Joe Christmas: Character Through Voice," *University of Texas Studies in Literature and Language*, II (Winter, 1961), 419-43.

19. Faulkner said to Cynthia Grenier, "Ratliff is wonderful. He's done more things than any man I know. Why, I couldn't tell some of the things that man has done . . ." (*Accent*, XVI [Summer, 1956], 174-75).

20. Albert Gérard, "Justice in Yoknapatawpha County . . ." *Faulkner Studies*, II (Winter, 1954), 54.

21. In this connection, see Andrew Lytle, "The Son of Man: He Will Prevail," *Sewanee Review*, LXIII (May, 1955), 114-37.

22. *The Reivers* (New York, 1962) testifies further to Faulkner's ability to put the human condition above abstractions.

23. That Yoknapatawpha has become both a famous world and an object of extravagant curiosity (exceeding even the world of Balzac's *Comédie Humaine*) is testified to by an amazing development in Faulkner criticism; within a few months of 1964, as many as six books appeared (called variously, *Handbook, Glossary, Who's Who, Reader's Guide*, etc.) each of which was dedicated mainly to giving information concerning the County and its inhabitants. The end of this development is not yet at hand. The initial incentive was a good one; but competition, as always in Faulkner scholarship, inspired repetition, and we now have a number of books which give approximately the same information.

Notes and References

Chapter Two

1. See Anderson's "A Meeting South," in *The Sherwood Anderson Reader* (Boston: Houghton Mifflin, 1947), pp. 274-84, for an imaginary account of his memories of Faulkner in New Orleans. Only *Soldiers' Pay* was written at this time, though the idea of *Mosquitoes* must also have come from it. The first book-length publication was a volume of derivative poems, called *The Marble Faun*, published by the Seven Seas Co. in 1924, and subsidized by Faulkner's Oxford friend, attorney Phil Stone. See Harry Runyan, *A Faulkner Glossary* (New York, 1964), pp. 197-203.

2. *The Novels of William Faulkner* (Baton Rouge, 1959), p. 8. Hereafter referred to in text as *Novels*.

3. *Mosquitoes* (New York: Liveright, 1927), p. 210.

4. Introduction to *Sartoris* (New York: Signet Books, 1953), pp. viii-ix.

5. *Sartoris* (New York: Harcourt, Brace, 1929), pp. 374-75.

Chapter Three

1. When speaking of the "fifth time," Faulkner is referring to the appendix he wrote of the Compson family history for Malcolm Cowley's edition of the *Portable Faulkner*. It was published in 1946, seventeen and not fifteen years after *The Sound and the Fury*. The appendix has the value of a kind of very somber retrospective meditation, and above all it gives the impression of the creator surveying all his creatures and the world into which he put them.

2. *Stream of Consciousness in The Modern Novel* (University of California Press, 1954), p. 105. For an excellent, thorough, and detailed summary of the action and the time scheme in *SF*, see Edmond L. Volpe's fine book, *A Reader's Guide to William Faulkner* (New York, 1964), pp. 353-77.

3. See *Three Decades*, pp. 16-17, for some contemporary reactions. Of course, the book has long since won its battle of acceptance. It is one of the most widely read, and taught, of Faulkner's novels, and perhaps (along with *Absalom, Absalom!* and *Light in August*) the most thoroughly researched. See *Three Decades*, pp. 422-24, for a list of essays on it; perhaps an extreme example of the types of scholarship used on *SF* is such an essay as this: George R. Stewart and Joseph M. Backus, " 'Each in Its Ordered Place': Structure and Narrative in 'Benjy's Section' of *The Sound and the Fury*," *American Literature*, XXIX (January, 1958), 440-56. Taking its cue from the very last five words of the novel, the authors (plus

eight students of "English 208" at Berkeley), provide charts and maps to indicate movements both in space and time in Part One.

4. The original is in italics, and generally speaking Faulkner intended italics to indicate a shift from one time fragment to another. See Lawrence Bowling, *Kenyon Review*, X (Autumn, 1948), 552-66, for a study of this and other matters of Faulkner's technique (also in *William Faulkner: Two Decades of Criticism* [East Lansing, Mich., 1951], pp. 165-79). Note that Faulkner, in his remarks to Mrs. Stein, replaces the pear tree with a rainpipe, as Miss Quentin's means of escape. There is every reason to believe that Faulkner wanted to help the reader through the device of italics as an indication; but it is not consistently employed. Whether he was serious when he proposed to print the different times in different colors and shades (he would have needed about thirteen) is less certain. For his remark about this latter plan, see *Faulkner at Nagano*, ed. by Robert A. Jelliffe (Tokyo, 1956), pp. 105-6.

5. That is, it will be a hell of their choosing, in which they are fully aware of their crime, like the position of Paolo and Francesca of Dante's *Inferno*. For a discussion of the sexual symbolism and imagery, see H. M. Campbell and Ruel Foster, *William Faulkner* (Norman, Okla., 1951), pp. 50-56.

5A. From all appearances, Quentin receives the wedding announcement about April 18 or 19, 1910, does not act upon it for three days, finally leaves for Jefferson, where he meets Herbert Head on April 22, two days before the wedding.

6. On this question, Edwin Berry Burgum speaks of Jason's unpleasant character but is moved as well to admire him (*The Novel and the World's Dilemma*, New York: Oxford University Press, 1947): ". . . we begin to realize that behind this contemptible surface . . . is a savage obsession to patch the walls of Usher, at last without doubt crumbling. He and he alone of the entire family is making some attempt to restore what they were once proud of in the past . . ." (209). This is of course true only in the most literal and superficial sense. With an almost complete record of Yoknapatawpha now available, it is possible to see Jason for what he is, by comparing him with the several kinds of Snopes. He is not the equal of Flem, who would have despised him for his hasty, frantic actions and his frequent attempts "morally" to justify what he does; above all, Flem would have held him in contempt because Jason was caught in a web of his own making, caused by an unpardonable-succession of oversights and unclever maneuvers.

7. This passage is from section four and is from Faulkner's own point of view; hence the third-person narration.

8. Several critics have made much of superficial parallels. One

of the better considerations of this question is Sumner C. Powell's "William Faulkner Celebrates Easter, 1928," *Perspective*, II (Summer, 1949), 195-218. See also "Introduction" to my *Three Decades*, pp. 35-36. See also Faulkner's own remark, one of several on the subject, in *Faulkner in the University*, p. 68: ". . . I'm quite sure it was quite instinctive that I picked out Easter, that I wasn't writing any symbolism of the Passion Week at all. . . ."

9. See Lawrence Bowling, *Two Decades*, p. 179: "The disorder, disintegration, and absence of perspective in the lives of the Compsons is intended to be symbolic and representative of a whole social order, or perhaps it would be better to say a whole social disorder." Perhaps the best answer to the question is given by Cleanth Brooks, in *William Faulkner: The Yoknapatawpha Country* (New Haven, 1963), p. 334.

10. *As I Lay Dying* (New York: Modern Library, 1946), p. 531. Originally published, New York, Cape and Smith, 1930. Hereafter referred to in text as *Dying*. See Volpe, *Reader's Guide*, pp. 377-82, for a useful, straightforward summary of the action. The burial takes place after nine days; on the tenth, Anse appears with Addie's successor.

11. As mentioned by Joseph Blotner, in *Twentieth Century Literature*, III (April, 1957), 14.

12. Peabody is also a part of the "other world" of Faulkner's work; he also appears in *Sartoris*, and is, as a doctor, a link of one class with another.

Chapter Four

1. Introduction to *Sanctuary* (New York: Modern Library, 1932), p. v. This edition has the advantage of the special Introduction. It is also identical in every detail with the first edition. In *Faulkner in the University*, (pp. 90-91), he seemed most apologetic about the novel. It was, he said, "basely conceived." When he'd been married (1929), ". . . I couldn't do things [like running a bootlegging boat or serving as a commercial airplane pilot], so I thought I would make a little money writing a book. . . ." Actually, *Sanctuary* was the beginning of affluence for him. It is one of those minor ironies of the literary life that a book he seemed often to be ashamed of (and, in *Requiem for a Nun*, apparently wanted to atone for) was the beginning of popular success. For one thing, it began his visits to Hollywood (November, 1932); on this occasion, he adapted it for Joan Crawford, in a film called *The Story of Temple Drake*. He went to Hollywood periodically thereafter, whenever he needed to pay for some large purchase. The 1932 Introduction can by no means be taken literally; nor can his

remarks at the University of Virginia (which came at least twenty-seven years after he'd written the first manuscript of *Sanctuary*). See Volpe, *Reader's Guide*, pp. 140-41 fn.

    2. See Introduction to *Three Decades*, pp. 17-18.

    3. *Faulkner in the University*, p. 91.

    4. It is interesting to see what happened to the story of *Sanctuary* as seen from the perspective of *Requiem for a Nun* (1951), published twenty years later. There is a lapse of eight years in the affairs of Temple Drake. Gavin Stevens replaces Benbow; he says exactly what Benbow had said, "that there is a corruption even in just looking at evil, even by accident" (New York: Random House, 1951, p. 129; cf. *Sanctuary*, p. 152), but he acts very differently about it. Temple Drake puts the entire burden of her "sin" upon herself; once having been corrupted by Popeye, she had chosen to stay in the Memphis brothel, though she could have escaped it at any time. The strategy of the later novel is to make the vicious cruelty of Popeye a matter of personal moral responsibility, so that Stevens can win over Temple Drake to an acknowledgment of it. The differences between the two novels can support (and have supported) some interesting speculations. Volpe (*Reader's Guide*) says of *Requiem* that it "focuses upon those moral and philosophical aspects of *Sanctuary* that are obscured for many readers by the sensationalism and the violence. The earlier novel depicts human evil as a manifestation of cosmic evil. The later book returns the responsibility for evil to man and places upon him the burden of his own salvation..." (p. 265). These shrewd remarks are, of course, a quite plausible interpretation of the difference between the Faulkner of 1930 and the "humanist" of 1951. Nevertheless, it is of some advantage to suppose that in 1930 (date of the first manuscript of *Sanctuary*) Faulkner was at least as much interested in particularizing his moral convictions. Benbow significantly "disappears," to all intents and purposes, in the 1950's; and he is replaced by Gavin Stevens. Both are lawyers; but their convictions radically differ concerning the moral power and the persuasive tactics not only of the lawyer, but of the secular theologian. Note, for example, that Stevens' attempt to persuade Temple Drake (it is interesting also that she is now Mrs. [Gowan] Stevens) takes place in the governor's office ("Act Two," pp. 240 ff.), and that the *décor* is relevantly "softened" (darkness interrupted by lights playing upon the principals). The very fact that the two novels differ radically in structure is pertinent (in *Sanctuary*, Benbow is maneuvered by an omniscient narrator; in the later novel, Stevens is allowed a dramatic center, a rostrum almost as powerfully helpful and flattering as that given Eliot's Thomas à Becket).

I believe that Benbow suffers not so much from what Cleanth Brooks calls the fate of being "the man of academic mind" (see *William Faulkner*, 116) who "finds out that the world is not a place of justice and moral tidiness" (though this is an excellent summary of his experience), but rather from the failure of the over-simple "liberal, idealist" conception of the moral hero. The failure of Benbow demonstrates that Faulkner was (in spite of his being "embarrassed" by the novel) a shrewd analyst of the liberal mind. That Benbow is also "untidy" in his personal life is an important additional insight: not that the two characteristics *necessarily* go together, but that the initial stance of what Volpe calls "idealism" (*Reader's Guide*, 407) is unreal and ingenuous. This situation suggests that liberal idealism is a major sympton of the modern "sickness." From John Dewey to Nelson Rockefeller, the "liberal" mind has frequently (and just barely) failed to understand the reasons and the circumstances of liberal inadequacy. We live in a "post-liberal" world and no convincing or even sensible rationale explaining modern terrors and violence, or accounting for them by means of a rhetoric we can accept has emerged. Benbow is, within the framework of this kind of discussion, a truly helpless person, all the more so because he scarcely knows what is happening to him, nor why he is causing it to happen.

5. "The Stillness of *Light in August*," in *Three Decades*, pp. 247-65. Originally in *Twelve Original Essays*, edited by Charles Shapiro (Detroit: Wayne State University Press, 1958), pp. 257-83.

6. See Olga W. Vickery, *Novels*, p. 70.

7. See O'Connor, *Tangled Fire*, pp. 72-87, the best study of this problem.

8. Note this remark about Faulkner and Hawthorne: "Both novels, *The Scarlet Letter* and *Light in August*, are concerned with the excesses of the thoroughly moralized imagination, and they are peopled, for the most part, by men and women committed to a vision of human conduct that is dark with a guilt that is not to be forgiven." William Van O'Connor, "Hawthorne and Faulkner," *Virginia Quarterly Review*, XXXIII (Winter, 1957), 113. Volpe (*Reader's Guide*, p. 164), speaks of Joe Christmas's "life-long struggle to establish his identity..." An interesting comparison and or contrast, in the light of this suggestion, might be made between *Light in August* and Ralph Ellison's *Invisible Man* (1952), with these exceptions: Joe Christmas does not actually have Negro blood, but takes on the harsh assignment his associates force on him; *Invisible Man* is in many ways a comic version of the Negro effort to adapt and adjust to his circumstances.

9. See *Three Decades*, pp. 278-304. Originally published in *PMLA*, LXX (December, 1955), 887-912. Much has been done

with the word "innocence," as it is used by Quentin Compson's grandfather: "Sutpen's trouble was innocence" (220). The word may mean simply *naïveté*, or it may point to the sudden change from a *state* of innocence (in the beginning, he lived where "the land belonged to anybody and everybody," [221]) to a point where he *has* to do what he *wants* to do, ambition and "design" coalescing absolutely. Quentin is reporting his grandfather (as his father had no doubt reported him); so there are at least three generations of puzzling and explaining and trying to understand. On p. 263, the word *innocence* receives another explanation: ". . . that innocence which believed that the ingredients of morality were like the ingredients of pie or cake and once you had measured them and balanced them and mixed them and put them into the oven it was all finished and nothing but pie or cake could come out. . . ." The terms of this "innocence" are not unlike those John Crowe Ransom gives to what he calls the "economic" motive, as distinguished from the esthetic. (See "Forms and Citizens," in *The World's Body* [New York: Scribner's, 1938], pp. 29-54, and especially pp. 32-33.) The point of all this probably is that Sutpen's experience at the door of the wealthy man in the Tidelands gave him no real time or opportunity (or that he took neither) to judge morally the change from one condition to another, and that he therefore continues to act without a sense of the consequences of his acts for anyone but himself.

10. Olga Vickery says: "For better or worse, Sutpen does reflect both the virtues and the vices of the South, but he does it without any of the social graces, the courtly gestures of the Sartorises" (*Novels*, 93). Faulkner's explanation of Sutpen (*Faulkner in the University*, 35) is relatively simple. Sutpen, he said, wanted "revenge" on the man whose servant turned him away from the front door: ". . . he also wanted to establish the fact that man is immortal; that man if he is man, cannot be inferior to another man through artificial standards or circumstances. . . . He said, I'm going to be the one that lives in the big house. I'm going to establish a dynasty, I don't care how, and he violated all the roles of decency and honor and pity and compassion, and the fates took revenge on him. . . ."

Chapter Five

1. "Folklore of the Air," *The American Mercury*, XXXVI (November, 1935), 370-72, a review of Jimmy Collins' *Test Pilot*. For Faulkner's early interest in flying, see the sketch, "Landing in Luck," published in *The Mississippian* for November 26, 1919, and reprinted in Carvel Collins, ed., *Early Prose and Poetry* (Boston, 1962), pp. 42-50. The piece was first published in a column edited

by Professor Irwin and called "Weekly Short Story." See Collins, 125-27.

2. *Modern Fiction Studies*, III (Winter, 1957-58), 305. Marvin's essay is in *Faulkner Studies*, I (Summer, 1952), 20-23. For the *Waste Land* parallels, see Hyatt Waggoner, *William Faulkner* (Lexington, Ky., 1959), pp. 126-32.

3. The best study of *The Unvanquished* is in Hyatt Waggoner's *William Faulkner: From Jefferson to the World*, pp. 170-83. It is a very fine and a correct consideration of the book's meaning.

4. The most convincing argument for their meaningful relationship is Joseph Moldenhauer's, in *Three Decades*, pp. 305-22. It is significant that the crucial acts in the two stories are related to each other by contrasting approaches to life: in the one, Harry Wilbourne is committed to prison because his unsuccessful abortion has led to Charlotte's death; in the other the tall convict rescues a pregnant woman, and in fact has to assist at the birth. He returns after seven weeks of journey, and announces simply, "Yonder's your boat, and here's the woman. But I never did find that bastard on the cottonhouse" (*Wild Palms*, New York: Random House, 1939, p. 278). Joseph Moldenhauer believes that Wilbourne is unable to enjoy "the pagan freedom Charlotte offers him..." that he therefore "follows a course of frenzied self-punishment which culminates in his blundering and compulsive murder of Charlotte" (*Three Decades*, 309). In a sense, he and the tall convict perform their acts (the one of killing two lives, the other of saving two) for approximately the same reasons. The convict does what he does because of the deputy's orders, and is glad to be back in the prison after his adventure.

5. *The Hamlet* (New York: Modern Library Paperbacks, 1956), pp. 4-5.

6. In this connection, Faulkner's remarks at the University of Virginia are relevant. Speaking of Flem's desire for respectability in *The Town*, he said that "rapacious people—if they're not careful—they are reduced away and decide that what they've got to have is respectability, which destroys one, almost anybody...." A first-rate scoundrel, "like a first-rate artist, he's an individualist, and the pressure's all against being an individualist..." (*Faulkner in the University*, 32, 33). But later he pointed out: "I never did feel sorry for him any more than one feels sorry for anyone who is ridden with an ambition or demon as base as simple vanity and rapacity and greed. I think that you can be ridden by a demon, but let it be a good demon..." (120).

7. *William Faulkner: A Critical Appraisal*, p. 104.

8. The best study of this aspect of *The Hamlet* is T. Y. Greet's in *Three Decades*, pp. 330-47; originally in *PMLA*, LXXII (Sep-

tember, 1957), 775-90. Cleanth Brooks (*William Faulkner*, 407-410) takes strong issue with Greet's interpretation because, he says, it "takes its method to extremes." Yet, while there may be a forcing of analogies here and there, Greet's essay seems to me to have the great merit of its planning, and it suggests a design in *The Hamlet* that is otherwise difficult to find.

9. Education is for him "an actual counterpart of the old monk's faith in his wooden cross" (118). On the other hand, Eula is the soul of passivity, neither wanting nor needing to know. Labove "took one look at her and saw what her brother [Jody] would doubtless be the last to discern. He saw that she not only was not going to study, but there was nothing in books here or anywhere else that she would ever need to know, who had been born already completely equipped not only to face and combat but to overcome anything the future could invent to meet her with" (114).

10. See Campbell and Foster, *William Faulkner*, p. 198. But Brooks, in his usual campaign for "common sense," refuses to see an analogy between the departure of Eula, the farcically elaborate and ironic love game of Ike and Houston's cow, and the deprivation of nature. Speaking against Greet's interpretation of *The Hamlet*, he says: "But it just isn't true to say that the cow beloved by Ike is the last vestige in the land of the shape of love. Eula is still in the land and so are a good many things, including other cows. As for the earth sterile 'in the grip of winter,' no redemptive act of love needs to be performed. Nature will take care of that: 'If winter comes, can spring be far behind?'" (*William Faulkner*, 410).

11. *The Mansion* (New York, 1959), pp. 415-16. The only book-length study of the *Snopes* trilogy (as Faulkner came to call the three volumes in *The Town* and *The Mansion*) is *Man in Motion*, by Warren Beck (Madison, Wis., 1961). There are, of course, changes from one volume to the next (perhaps some of them are errors); the length of time from *The Hamlet* (1940), and the events intervening (the Nobel Award, and the publication of *Requiem*, 1951 and *A Fable*, 1954) probably account for some of the changes. Most important are the growth in "sophistication" of people like Eula (whose character changes radically); the entrance of such people as Gavin Stevens, Chick Mallison (see *Intruder*), and Eula's daughter Linda (who has her own special reasons for hating him) into the campaign against Flem; and a further and sharper differentiation among Snopeses, so that at the end of the trilogy Flem stands out as a master villain—not uniquely, for other Snopeses have emulated him, but elaborately. Speaking at Washington and Lee University (*Faulkner in the University*, 283), he said

that "Snopes will evolve into what you might say an accepted type of Snopes. Either that or he'll have to vanish. . . ." Another aspect of the trilogy has to do with the translation of short story into novel, especially in the case of *The Hamlet*. The following appeared first in magazines as stories (except when otherwise noted, these eventually appeared in *The Hamlet*): "Spotted Horses" (*Scribner's*, LXXXIX, June, 1931); "The Hound" (*Harper's*, CLXIII, August, 1931; also in *Doctor Martino*); "Centaur in Brass" (*American Mercury*, XXV, February, 1932; revised for *The Town*); "Lizards in Jamshyd's Courtyard," (*Saturday Evening Post*, CCIV, February 27, 1932); "Mule in the Yard" (*Scribner's*, CLVI, August, 1934; revised for *The Town*); "Fool About a Horse" (*Scribner's*, C, August, 1936); "Barn Burning," (*Harper's*, CLXXIX, June, 1939, the central episode revised for *The Hamlet*); "By the People," (*Mademoiselle*, XLI, October, 1955; revised for *The Mansion*). The above information, as well as other useful facts concerning the process of "building" from short story to novel, is to be found in Harry Runyan's *A Faulkner Glossary* (New York, 1964), pp. 220-35.

12. *Moses*, 193.

13. His grandfather had seduced and had a child by a Negress slave, Tomasina, who may well also have been his own daughter. Ike has therefore to consider the twin horrors of incest and miscegenation. For a discussion of the complicated McCaslin family relationships, as well as a genealogy, consult Volpe (*Reader's Guide*), pp. 230-52; Runyan (*Glossary*), pp. 258-65; and Dorothy Tuck (*Crowell's Handbook of William Faulkner*, New York, 1964), pp. 95-106. For an excellent discussion of the place of the Negro in Faulkner's work, see Charles Nilon, *Faulkner and the Negro*, *University of Colorado Studies*, No. 8, September, 1962. F. L. Utley, L. Z. Bloom, and A. F. Kinney, have put together materials relevant to "The Bear," in *Bear, Man, and God* (New York, 1964).

14. He is speaking of the last two lines of Stanza 2 of the "Ode on a Grecian Urn": "She cannot fade, though thou hast not thy bliss, Forever wilt thou love, and she be fair."

15. See the reaction of Mr. Lilley, the smalltime grocer: "All he requires is that they act like niggers" (48). Again, the whites say if Lucas had only said "mister" to them, they would have accepted him (62). In (or near) the end, Faulkner has Gavin Stevens sum up the implications of Lucas's firm and successful stand in the face of the accusation of murder and the danger of a lynching: ". . . we shall watch right here in Yoknapatawpha County the ancient oriental relationship between the savior and the life he saved turned upside down: Lucas Beauchamp once the slave of any white man within range of whose notice he happened to come, now

tyrant over the whole country's white conscience...." (*Intruder*, 199).

16. In the revised version of his book (1962), this statement seems to have disappeared, though Howe's animadversions regarding the Stevens rhetoric persist. He admits (pp. 99-100 fn.) that Faulkner "negotiates a certain ironic distance" from Stevens in certain novels; but this it not true, alas, of *Intruder*, where "Stevens is so clearly admired in his role of *raisonneur*." Once again, one needs to invoke the idea or theory of the "voice"; it is true that the effectiveness of it is here all but lost, but I suppose Faulkner should be given the protection of the quotation marks he puts around Stevens's worst rhetorical offenses.

Chapter Six

1. *Faulkner Studies*, I (Summer, 1952), 18.

2. John Maclachlan maintained that Faulkner's County (and its equivalent in reality) was responsible for the success of his work because "There is nothing between its folk and the elemental forces of the universe, no canopies, walls, clinics, ranks of professionals and bureaucrats to stand between them and life and death." *Southern Renaissance*, edited by Louis D. Rubin, Jr., and Robert D. Jacobs (Baltimore: Johns Hopkins Press, 1953), p. 107.

3. Durham: Duke University Press, 1955, p. 145. Harry Runyan (*Glossary*) lists some thirteen addresses, the first of which was the Stockholm speech, December 10, 1950 (208-10). It is significant that this date marks Faulkner's first public appearance, in the fifty-third year of his life; also, we may note a radical change from the private to the public man, marked by such volumes of commentary as *Faulkner at Nagano* (1956), and *Faulkner at West Point* (New York, 1964). There is much repetition of ideas here, but the important fact is his growth of self-confidence and the effect of his being in the limelight on his rhetoric. Runyan lists nine interviews, and points out that he is acknowledging only "those interviews and conferences of some length which have a sense of completeness about them" (217-18). Only *Time* magazine thought Faulkner of sufficient importance before 1950 to make a public personage of him; see the "cover story" of an issue in January, 1939. The occasion was a review of *The Wild Palms*, one of the least discussed of his novels.

4. See *Three Decades*, pp. 347-48, for the full text.

5. See *Go Down, Moses*, p. 297.

6. If any proof were needed of the consistency of Faulkner's public statements, his remarks in Japan are more than adequate; here he says that the belief that man will prevail "is like the belief

that one has in God, Buddha. . . ." Man is immortal because he has survived "in spite of all the anguishes and griefs which he himself has invented and seems to continue to invent." (*Faulkner at Nagano*, 27, 28).

7. See *Three Decades*, pp. 123. Originally in the *New Republic*, August 12 and 26, 1946, as a review of the *Portable Faulkner*. Since Warren's essay, several speculations concerning the "voice" have appeared, none of them more convincing than Sister Kristin Morrison's "Faulkner's Joe Christmas: Character through Voice," *University of Texas Studies in Language and Literature*, II (Winter, 1961), 419-43. I find this statement especially persuasive: "Faulkner . . . frequently represents throughout his work not the literal mind-voice of a character but a heightened voice: a voice that is rooted in the mind of the character, a voice that issues from that mind yet is not bound by the limits of intelligence and sensibility which that mind has by nature, a voice heightened to perception and articulation of which the mind itself is incapable . . ." (426).

This suggestion seems to me capable of starting a new series of critical observations. Of course, one would have to determine the limits of the "voice": that is, the points beyond which Faulkner allows his "voice" to overwhelm his character, to blur the outlines of a personality. This condition is possibly true of parts of *Intruder* and *Requiem*. If Sister Kristin's observations have merit, we shall, by pressing them further, be able to find a type of rhetoric which enables a novelist to escape the "tar pits" and "slag heaps" of naturalism. One should note at least two other devices in the history of the novel: that in which the novelist keeps an ironic reserve with respect to his characters, to protect himself from implication in their inanities or their limitations (Stendhal, Flaubert); that in which the novelist deliberately chooses characters of fine intelligence, so that he may speak without embarrassment through them (James).

8. "Gavin Stevens: From Rhetoric to Dialectic," *Faulkner Studies*, II (Spring, 1953), 4.

9. Faulkner explains Nancy as the "nun" in this way: ". . . she was capable within her poor dim lights and reasons of an act which whether it was right or wrong was of complete almost religious abnegation of the world for the sake of an innocent child. That was—it was paradoxical, the use of the word *Nun* for her, but I—but to me that added something to her tragedy" (*Faulkner in the University*, 196). That is, a "nun" in this context is a "moral heroine," capable of an extraordinary act, whether to "teach" or to save someone other than herself. The *idea* of moral heroism underwent a quite radical change in Faulkner's last years.

The "verities" of the Stockholm address are used more and more frequently as directive means. The moral hero is a *secular* hero; there is nothing distinctively "theological" (in the sense of offering evidence of any link to divinity in his acts) in what he does; rather, his acts are in the nature of a triumph of the "heart" over the "glands."

10. *Requiem for a Nun: A Play*, by William Faulkner, with Ruth Ford (New York: Random House, 1959). Also Albert Camus adapted it for the French stage: *Requiem pour une nonne* (Paris: Gallimard, 1956).

11. *Requiem for a Nun* (New York, 1951), p. 283. Hereafter referred to in text as *Requiem*.

12. *A Fable* (New York, 1954), p. 354. See Volpe (*Reader's Guide*), pp. 396-401, for a chronology of events, especially needed in this case. The general reaction to *A Fable* has been unfavorable, on several grounds. Irving Howe, in the revised edition of his *William Faulkner* (1962), calls it "an example of the yearning so common to American writers for a 'big book,' a *summa* of vision and experience, a final spilling-out of the wisdom of the heart. . . . [It is], one regretfully concludes, still another of those 'distinguished' bad books that flourish in America" (268-69). Strangely, in his vast and detailed work of 1963, Cleanth Brooks has only one reference to *A Fable* (*William Faulkner*, 367): "In *A Fable* the attempt to make a case for certain human values led to allegorical abstractions, which again involve oversimplifications." Of course, the subtitle of his book (*The Yoknapatawpha Country*) is enough to explain the omission; still, *Requiem for a Nun*, which *is* Yoknapatawphan in setting, gets very little more mention.

13. See *Faulkner in the University*, pp. 17, 68, 86, and especially pp. 117-18.

14. *Sewanee Review*, LXIII (Winter, 1955), 115.

15. *Kenyon Review*, XVI (Autumn, 1954), 622.

16. *Review of Politics*, XVIII (January, 1956), 65.

17. *College English*, XVI (May, 1955), 475.

18. See Brooks, p. 448, and Volpe (*Reader's Guide*), p. 231, for McCaslin genealogies.

19. *The Reivers* (New York, 1962), p. 302. *Reivers* is an archaic word, meaning "plunderers."

Chapter Seven

1. Or sixteen. The number depends upon whether or not one is persuaded that *The Unvanquished* and *Go Down, Moses* are novels or "collections of short stories" connected by "certain

dominant themes." This issue is idle or "academic" (in the quaint use of the latter term to indicate the sense of "unreal").

2. Or *all but* completed work. Faulkner said he had destroyed the manuscripts of three novels with which he said he was not satisfied. Beyond these, there will be manuscripts *not* destroyed (or rumored still to exist) and fragments among the papers. Also, the editing of texts goes on, and details will be changed in the novels as they now exist; the result of this editing will have to be called the "posthumous Faulkner."

3. Margaret Patricia Ford and Suzanne Kincaid, *Who's Who in Faulkner* (Baton Rouge, 1963); Robert W. Kirk and Marvin Klotz, *Faulkner's People: A Complete Guide and Index to Characters in the Fiction of William Faulkner* (Berkeley and Los Angeles, 1963); Harry Runyan, *A Faulkner Glossary;* The Dictionary of Characters in Dorothy Tuck's *Handbook* (pp. 183-229); and the "Character Index" in Brooks's *William Faulkner* (pp. 453-87). All of these except Runyan's books have genealogical tables as well.

4. I am indebted to Harry Runyan, who in his *Glossary* (Appendix V, pp. 238-83) describes the histories of the principal Yoknapatawpha families.

5. See "Chronology," above, and biographical sketches by Robert Cantwell (in *Three Decades,* 51-66), as well as in Runyan's *Glossary* and Miss Tuck's *Handbook.*

6. See the interview with Jean Stein, *Three Decades,* pp. 73-74.

7. "Appendix" to SF, p. 16. See Runyan, pp. 251-52, for the conflicting accounts of the early Compson history.

8. See Ward and Kincaid, *Who's Who,* pp. 89-94.

9. See above, chapter 1, pp. 24-32.

10. *Absalom, Absalom!,* p. 31.

11. See *Faulkner in the University,* pp. 90-91.

12. In the essay, "Faulkner's Joe Christmas: Character through Voice," cited above several times.

13. In the Modern Library edition.

14. I suppose only Southern Californians will understand the reference. I have in mind a neon sign I once saw at that spot, on the top of a bank (not Casey Stengel's), which read: "Jesus Saves. Why Don't You?"

15. See, once again, that passage at the end of Faulkner's interview with Jean Stein: ". . . The fact that I have moved my characters around in time successfully, at least in my own estimation, proves to me my own theory that time is a fluid condition which has no existence except in the momentary avatars of individual people . . ." (*Three Decades,* 82).

16. See, for example, the opening paragraphs of Section Four of *The Sound and the Fury* (281-82) and the actual words at Dilsey's

command. The two powerfully support and reinforce each other.

17. A brilliant illustration is to be found in the "Old Man" chapters of *The Wild Palms*. The tall convict is quite incapable of elaborating his reactions, and in any case quite unwilling to do so. Faulkner has quite effectively aided him, without in any way interfering with him:

> ... It was mud he lay upon, but it was solid underneath [This is simple narration], it was earth, it did not move [This is a statement the convict can "sense" rather than say; in any case, he is not given to much "saying"]; if you fell upon it you broke your bones against its incontrovertible passivity sometimes, but it did not accept you substanceless and enveloping and suffocating, down and down and down [This is obviously beyond the convict's power to state, but not beyond his power to *feel*. Faulkner is *telling us* how the convict feels, because the convict cannot communicate it to us; but the feeling is genuine in either case]; it was hard at times to drive a plow through, it sent you spent, weary, and cursing its light-long insatiable demands, back to your bunk at sunset at times, but it did not snatch you violently out of all familiar knowing and sweep you, thrall and impotent, for days against any returning ..." (*The Wild Palms,* 232-33).

Selected Bibliography

Selected Bibliography

WORKS BY FAULKNER

The Marble Faun. Boston: The Four Seas Co., 1924.
Soldiers' Pay. New York: Boni and Liveright, 1926.
Mosquitoes. New York: Boni and Liveright, 1927.
Sartoris. New York: Harcourt, Brace and Co., 1929.
The Sound and the Fury. New York: Jonathan Cape and Harrison Smith, 1929.
As I Lay Dying. New York: Cape and Smith, 1930.
Sanctuary. New York: Cape and Smith, 1939.
These Thirteen. New York: Cape and Smith, 1931.
Light in August. New York: Harrison Smith and Robert Haas, 1932.
Salmagundi. Edited by Paul Romaine. Milwaukee: Casanova Press, 1932 (contains five poems and three essays).
A Green Bough. New York: Smith and Haas, 1933.
Doctor Martino and Other Stories. New York: Smith and Haas, 1934.
Pylon. New York: Smith and Haas, 1935.
Absalom, Absalom! New York: Random House, 1936.
The Unvanquished. New York: Random House, 1938.
The Wild Palms. New York: Random House, 1939.
The Hamlet. New York: Random House, 1940. Also in New York: The Modern Library, 1956.
Go Down, Moses and Other Stories. New York: Random House, 1942. Also in New York: The Modern Library, 1955.
Intruder in the Dust. New York: Random House, 1948.
Knight's Gambit. New York: Random House, 1949.
Collected Stories of William Faulkner. New York: Random House, 1950.
Requiem for a Nun. New York: Random House, 1951.
A Fable. New York: Random House, 1954.
Big Woods. New York: Random House, 1955.
The Town. New York: Random House, 1957.
New Orleans Sketches, ed. by Carvel Collins. New Brunswick, New Jersey: Rutgers University Press, 1958.
The Mansion. New York: Random House, 1959.
The Reivers. New York: Random House, 1962.
Early Prose and Poetry, ed. by Carvel Collins. Boston: Little, Brown, 1962.

STUDIES OF FAULKNER

NOTE: *Faulkner scholarship and criticism have increased so much that the list below has been expanded from the first edition. I include only books and pamphlets. Readers who wish to check essays can consult the second and third items of I, below.*

I. Bibliography and Check-lists

MERIWETHER, JAMES B. *The Literary Career of William Faulkner: A Bibliographical Study.* Princeton University Press, 1961. A record of the exhibition at the Princeton Library, 1957, with additions to the original article in the *Princeton University Library Chronicle,* of Spring, 1957.

SLEETH, IRENE L. *William Faulkner: A Bibliography of Criticism.* Denver: Alan Swallow, 1962. No. 13 of the Swallow Pamphlets.

VICKERY, OLGA W. "Bibliography," in *William Faulkner: Three Decades of Criticism.* East Lansing: The Michigan State University Press, 1960, pp. 393-422.

II. Handbooks, Glossaries, Indexes of Characters

FORD, MARGARET F., and SUZANNE KINCAID. *Who's Who in Faulkner.* Baton Rouge: Louisiana State University Press, 1963.

KIRK, ROBERT W., and MARVIN KLOTZ. *Faulkner's People: A Complete Guide and Index to Characters in the Fiction of William Faulkner.* Berkeley and Los Angeles: University of California Press, 1963.

RUNYAN, HARRY. *A Faulkner Glossary.* New York: Citadel Press, 1964.

TUCK, DOROTHY. *Crowell's Handbook of Faulkner.* New York: T. Y. Crowell, 1964.

VOLPE, EDMUND L. *A Reader's Guide to William Faulkner.* New York: Farrar, Straus, 1964.

NOTE: *Cleanth Brooks* (William Faulkner: The Yoknapatawpha Country, *New Haven, Yale University Press, 1963) has an Index of Characters, pp. 453-87.*

III. Collections of Interviews

FANT, JOSEPH L., and ROBERT ASHLEY, eds. *Faulkner at West Point.* New York: Random House, 1964. A short view of one of Faulkner's last public appearances.

Selected Bibliography

GWYNN, FREDERICK L., and JOSEPH BLOTNER, eds. *Faulkner in the University: Class Conferences at the University of Virginia, 1957-1958.* Charlottesville: University of Virginia, 1959. Perhaps the best of the collections of Faulkner's talks.

JELLIFFE, ROBERT A., ed. *Faulkner at Nagano.* Tokyo: Kenkyusha Ltd., 1956. Faulkner's remarks in Japan, August of 1955.

IV. Memoirs, Criticism, and Scholarship

BECK, WARREN. *Man in Motion: Faulkner's Trilogy.* Madison: University of Wisconsin Press, 1961. A study of *The Hamlet, The Town,* and *The Mansion.*

BROOKS, CLEANTH. *William Faulkner: The Yoknapatawpha Country.* New Haven: Yale University Press, 1963. A compendious account of all Yoknapatawpha books except *Requiem for a Nun.*

CAMPBELL, HARRY MODEAN, and RUEL E. FOSTER. *William Faulkner: A Critical Appraisal.* Norman: University of Oklahoma Press, 1951. The first critical study, this is still valuable.

COUGHLAN, ROBERT. *The Private World of William Faulkner: A Critical Appraisal.* New York: Harper and Bros., 1954. Some interesting anecdotes.

CULLEN, JOHN B., in collaboration with FLOYD C. WATKINS. *Old Times in the Faulkner Country.* Chapel Hill: The University of North Carolina Press, 1961. Local history.

FAULKNER, JOHN. *My Brother Bill: An Affectionate Reminiscence.* New York: Trident Press, 1963. An affecting account published shortly after Faulkner's death.

HICKERSON, THOMAS F. *The Falkner Feuds.* Chapel Hill: Colonial Press, 1964. Some events in the lives of Faulkner's ancestors.

HOFFMAN, FREDERICK J. *William Faulkner.* Revised edition. New York: Twayne, 1966. (First edition, 1961.)

–––––, and OLGA W. VICKERY, eds. *William Faulkner: Two Decades of Criticism.* East Lansing: Michigan State University Press, 1951. First edition, which contains essays by the following persons, not included in *Three Decades,* listed below: A. Wigfall Green, John Arthos, Rabi, Lawrence Bowling, Richard Chase, William Poirier, Elizabeth Hardwick, Andrew Lytle, and Ray B. West, Jr.

–––––, and OLGA W. VICKERY, eds. *William Faulkner: Three Decades of Criticism.* East Lansing: Michigan State University Press, 1960. Introduction, of 50 pages, by Hoffman, a survey of types of critical reception of Faulkner from its beginning to 1960. Contains essays by Robert Cantwell, Jean Stein (interview), G. M. O'Donnell, Malcolm Cowley, R. P.

Warren, Ursula Brumm, Conrad Aiken, Warren Beck, J. J. Mayoux, W. J. Slatoff, Florence Leaver, Lawrance Thompson, Jean-Paul Sartre, Olga Vickery, Alfred Kazin, John L. Langley, Ilse Dusoir Lind, W. V. O'Connor, T. Y. Greet, Heinrich Straumann, Philip Blair Rice, Steven Marcus, and the text of the Stockholm address.

Howe, Irving. *William Faulkner: A Critical Study.* New York: Vintage Books, 1962. Revised edition (first edition, New York, Random House, 1952). Revised edition includes discussion of a decade of Faulkner's works.

Longley, John L., Jr. *The Tragic Mask: A Study of Faulkner's Heroes.* Chapel Hill: University of North Carolina Press, 1963. Study of Faulkner in terms of certain parallels.

Malin, Irving. *William Faulkner: An Interpretation.* Stanford: Stanford University Press, 1957. An ineffectual attempt.

Millgate, Michael. *William Faulkner.* New York: Grove Press, 1961. (An Evergreen Pilot Book.) One of the better short studies.

Miner, Ward L. *The World of William Faulkner.* Durham: Duke University Press, 1952. Some analogies of fiction with fact.

Nilon, Charles H. *Faulkner and the Negro.* (University of Colorado Studies, Series in Language and Literature, No. 8.) Boulder: University of Colorado Press, 1962. A valuable study of one of the important Faulkner types.

O'Connor, William Van. *The Tangled Fire of William Faulkner.* Minneapolis: University of Minnesota Press, 1954. An early interpretation.

————, *William Faulkner.* Minneapolis: University of Minnesota Press, 1959. (No. 3 of University of Minnesota Pamphlets on American Writers.) Slight.

Robb, Mary C. *William Faulkner.* Pittsburgh: University of Pittsburgh Press, 1957. One of the poorest essays on Faulkner.

Slatoff, Walter. J. *Quest for Failure: A Study of William Faulkner.* Ithaca: Cornell University Press, 1960. An interesting study of Faulkner's rhetoric.

Swiggart, Peter. *The Art of Faulkner's Novels.* Austin: University of Texas Press, 1962. Puritans and others.

Thompson, Lawrance. *William Faulkner: An Introduction and Interpretation.* New York: Barnes and Noble, 1963. One of the better introductory statements.

Utley, F. L., L. Z. Bloom, and A. F. Kinney, eds. *Bear, Man and God: Seven Approaches to William Faulkner's "The Bear."* New York: Random House, 1964. A compendium and case book.

Selected Bibliography

VICKERY, OLGA W. *The Novels of William Faulkner: A Critical Interpretation.* Baton Rouge: Louisiana State University Press, 1965. Revised edition (first edition, 1959). New edition of the best critical study of Faulkner.

WAGGONER, HYATT H. *William Faulkner: From Jefferson to the World.* Lexington: University of Kentucky Press, 1959. A strangely tendentious book, whose best value lies in the study of *The Unvanquished.*

WOODWORTH, S. D. *William Faulkner in France: Panorama Critique, 1931-1952.* Paris: M. J. Minard, 1959. (A book in the *Lettres Modernes* series.) Some very interesting discussions of the problems involved in translating Faulkner.

Index

Index

Index